1986

# Teacher's Guide to Classroom Management

# TEACHER'S GUIDE TO CLASSROOM MANAGEMENT

Daniel Linden Duke
*Lewis and Clark College*

Adrienne Maravich
Meckel
*Stanford University*

Random House  New York

First Edition

9 8 7 6 5 4 3 2 1

Copyright © 1984 by Random House, Inc.

Library of Congress Cataloging in Publication Data

Duke, Daniel Linden.
    Teacher's guide to classroom management.

    Bibliography: p.
    Includes index.
    1. Classroom management. I. Meckel,
Adrienne Maravich. II. Title.
LB3013.D84      1983      371.1'024      83–4545
ISBN 0–394–32690–3

Manufactured in the United States of America

We dedicate this book to our parents, Gale Linden Duke and
Bonnie and John Maravich, for managing us so well; to new
arrivals Devan Elena and Moya Anne, for reminding us how important the future of teaching is; and to the Stanford Teacher
Education Program Class of 1981, for giving us hope in the profession.

# P·R·E·F·A·C·E

In the 1895 edition of David P. Page's *Theory and Practice of Teaching*, the author addresses a series of review questions to prospective teachers. One of the questions asks, "Why should teachers adopt plans specially adapted to their conditions and ability?" The answer: "Plans and methods must embody the teacher's ideals and be adapted to his individual characteristics and power."

We could not agree more. For this reason, we regard with concern the tendency of school officials, consultants, and teacher educators to compel teachers to learn and utilize a single "best" approach to teaching. Nowhere has this tendency been more pronounced than the area of classroom management, where dozens of approaches currently are purveyed to educators as panaceas.

It is our belief that the selection of an approach to classroom management is a decision best left to teachers. Further, we realize that the conditions of teaching change. These changes may occasion the choice of new approaches. Research on classroom management has not yet demonstrated that any particular approach to classroom management is most effective under all conditions. The fact that teachers grow older, change in temperament, acquire new skills, shift teaching assignments, teach different types of students, and work with different administrators means that they need to be aware of a variety of strategies for encouraging productive student behavior. It is to this purpose that *Teacher's Guide to Classroom Management* is dedicated.

Many useful books on classroom management have been published over the years since David Page's *Theory and Practice of Teaching*, but few have treated the teacher as an intelligent consumer of pedagogical ideas — an individual who, when provided with adequate information on a variety of options, is capable of selecting the most appropriate alternative. We have picked nine of the more distinctive approaches to classroom management and collected background data on each, together with descriptions of how each approach might be applied in a classroom setting. We also suggest some considerations for teachers to bear in mind as they decide which approach — if any — would be most useful.

We hope that others will emulate this format and present information to teachers in a way that facilitates teacher-based decisions. In the final analysis, no one is more aware of his or her teaching abilities, personal values, or working conditions than the individual teacher. The viability of the teaching profession is premised on the recognition of this fact. Telling teachers that they *must* manage their classrooms according to a certain prescription ignores the worth of professional judgment and reduces teaching to a semiskilled occupation. It is difficult for us to imagine attracting talented new teachers to the profession without acknowledging that teachers are decision makers capable of selecting or developing an appropriate classroom management plan.

Daniel Linden Duke
Portland, Oregon

Adrienne Maravich Meckel
Carmel Valley, California

January, 1983

# C·O·N·T·E·N·T·S

# PREPARING TO BE A CLASSROOM MANAGER

It would be difficult to find an issue in American public schooling that has generated more concern, criticism, and constructive effort over the past decade than student conduct — or what popularly is known as "discipline." Congressional subcommittees have debated the matter. Local and state task forces have been formed to generate ideas. Colleges and universities have attempted to modify their training programs. Professional organizations have demanded more technical support and administrative assistance. No group, however, has felt the pressure for improvements in student behavior more than classroom teachers.

Researchers in recent years have confirmed what conventional wisdom long has held: how teachers *think* about student behavior determines to a great extent how they *handle* student behavior. For example, teachers who believe they are in control of what goes on within their classrooms tend to be more effective classroom managers than teachers who feel powerless, overworked, and insecure. The first step in becoming an effective classroom manager — the major goal of this book — thus entails understanding how to think about students, their behavior, rules, punishments, the purposes of schools, and related subjects.

Taking time to clarify one's thinking is easier said than done. Teachers normally have more to do than time available for doing it. Still, there is no substitute for careful reflection. Without it, teachers frequently condemn themselves to repeat mistakes and minimize their chances of working effectively with students. Chapter 1 is designed to facilitate thinking about classroom management. Five basic assumptions are identified and discussed. Later, when specific approaches to managing classrooms are presented in Chapter 2, the identification of key assumptions underlying each approach serves as a primary component of analysis.

The assumption that gives rise to this book is that no one best way to manage classrooms has been found. No single set of practices works best for all students or for one student all of the time. Different grade levels and subject matter areas may call for different management strategies. Ultimately each teacher must select, adapt, or develop the approach that will work for him or her. To assist in this effort, we identify and summarize nine popular approaches to classroom management. In Part II, we illustrate how these approaches can be used to handle a variety of student behavior problems. The concluding portion of the book — Part III — provides guidelines to help teachers determine which approach is best suited to their own needs, beliefs, and abilities. We thus end as we began — by stressing the vital role of teacher thinking in effective classroom management.

# Thinking About Classroom Management

Late summer. Time for a final trip to the beach or the mountains. Time for enjoying the last moments of vacation before school begins. If you are a teacher, time for apprehension and anxiety. Have you planned your courses sufficiently? Will you arrive at school only to discover that the principal has reassigned you to three new courses? What will your students be like? Will they be interested in what you have to teach? Will they behave well enough to permit you to teach, or will you be forced to spend much of your time on discipline?

Many of the concerns that occupy teachers' thoughts are related to classroom management. What is classroom management? It refers to *the processes and provisions that are necessary to create and maintain environments in which teaching and learning can occur.* Classroom management encompasses everything from the allocation of time, space, and materials to record keeping. Probably the aspect of classroom management that receives the most attention, however, is the handling of student behavior problems — or what is popularly referred to as discipline. It is this topic to which this book is devoted.

Traditionally, most teachers have entered the profession because of their enjoyment of teaching subject matter and their commitment to helping young people. Many grow disillusioned, however, as they discover that a substantial amount of class time must be spent on noninstructional duties. One of the least liked of these duties — and one for which teachers have received the least training — is discipline. We hear teachers say, "But I never expected I would have to be a policeman in school!"

We believe that the best way to avoid becoming disillusioned is to avoid having illusions in the first place. We counsel prospective teachers to expect to devote time to handling student behavior problems. Anyone who enters teaching expecting only to instruct students has an unrealistic vision of the profession. No evidence of which we are aware suggests that there has ever been a time in the history of American schools when students did not behave in ways teachers thought were inappropriate. Thus, the first assumption on which this book is based is that classroom management, particularly the handling of student behavior problems, is an integral part of every teacher's responsibilities. As such, it should be an integral part of every teacher's training.

---

### Assumption No. 1
*Classroom management is an integral part of teaching.*

---

Maintaining that teachers should expect to encounter occasional student behavior problems is not to suggest, however, that teachers are helpless to minimize the frequency or severity of behavior problems. If we believed teachers could do nothing to reduce student behavior problems, there would be no point in writing this book. Research focusing on the behavior of more effective and less effective teachers clearly shows that certain teacher behaviors are related to fewer classroom management problems. In other words, great classroom managers are not necessarily born. Teachers can acquire specific skills to help them deal successfully with student behavior problems.

---

### Assumption No. 2
*Teachers can be trained to handle behavior problems effectively.*

---

At present no clear agreement prevails that one way to train teachers is best, however. The primary purpose of this book is to expose prospective and experienced teachers to a variety of approaches to classroom management. It is not essential for individuals to have taught in order to benefit from the book. The fact that prospective teachers once were students in elementary and secondary schools is sufficient to provide them with the background necessary to appreciate the numerous illustrations that follow. We offer this *Teacher's Guide to Classroom Management* in the spirit of a consumer's guide. Our hope is that by describing some of the major approaches and discussing their pros and cons, seasoned veterans and prospective teachers will find themselves in a better position to determine which is the most appropriate approach for them.

We want to underscore the fact that we are not attempting to "sell" any particular approach to classroom management. This disclaimer supports a third assumption on which the book is based — that teachers are in the best position to determine how they most effectively can manage their classrooms, assuming they have access to accurate information on the alternatives available. We intend to provide this information. It is our belief that administrators are mistaken to tell teachers what classroom management approach to use. Different teachers have different styles of operation. If an approach feels uncomfortable, it is unlikely to help a teacher deal more effectively with behavior problems.

---

## Assumption No. 3

*Teachers are in the best position to determine how they most effectively can manage their classrooms.*

---

A common problem for many teachers is that they are exposed to a new approach to classroom management in a course or a workshop without receiving any information on competing alternatives. Decision theorists contend that individuals are less likely to make a good decision when they consider only one or two alternatives. In the second chapter we shall introduce nine different approaches to managing student behavior problems. Each approach has been recognized by professional educators and implemented in schools. Chapters 3 through 8 focus on specific student behavior problems — from truancy to disrespect — and discuss how various approaches might handle them. Chapter 9 describes how to go about deciding on a useful approach for a particular teaching situation. The final chapter covers additional issues of importance to classroom management, including student rights and teacher stress.

Before continuing, we would like to ask you to think about how you plan to approach the reading of this book. What are your expectations? After all, if there is one finding on which most educational researchers agree it is that expectations exercise considerable influence over learning. Do you expect a practical guide to classroom management — such as this book purports to be — to be crammed full of tips and techniques that can be used tomorrow?

While we hope that you will discover many ideas that can be put to immediate use, our intention is less to help you *react* to specific behavior problems than to reflect on the purposes of classroom management. This focus derives from our concern that educators frequently are so busy dealing with day-to-day problems that they do not take time to think about their overall approach to classroom management. As a result, many teachers feel they are controlled by events in their classrooms, rather than being in charge themselves.

---

## Assumption No. 4

*Teachers often are so busy reacting to day-to-day problems that they fail to reflect on the purposes of classroom management.*

---

Many teachers find that adopting a comprehensive approach to classroom management helps them feel more in charge. Other advantages include *consistency, explanatory power,* and *security.*

When teachers simply react to problems as they arise, they are more likely to be influenced by such variables as mood, hour of the day, day of the week, student attitude, and current activity. Teachers who possess approaches to classroom management such as those introduced in the next chapter find it easier to deal with problems consistently. Furthermore, many researchers feel that teacher consistency may be a key element in effective classroom management.

A second reason for adopting a comprehensive approach to classroom management concerns situations in which teachers are required to explain or justify their behavior. The authors of each of the approaches discussed in this book have spent years developing explanations for the strategies they advocate. Should a teacher using one of these approaches be called upon by a parent or administrator to defend the way he handled a particular problem, he need only explain the rationale supporting his approach.

Teachers who possess no approach and who choose to deal with problems as they arise are less likely to provide convincing reasons for what they do.

Security is a third reason for selecting a comprehensive approach to classroom management. Serious difficulties can develop when a teacher is confronted by an unexpected behavior problem and reacts in a confused manner. What may start out as an incident involving a single student quickly can escalate and engulf an entire class. The likelihood of getting caught "off guard" is reduced by following one approach to classroom management. In the development of each of the nine approaches in this book, the authors have tried to anticipate unexpected problems and provide contingency plans for how to handle them. No teacher is ever completely protected from the occurrence of unexpected problems, but knowing in advance how to react to such events generally prevents these isolated incidents from getting out of control.

We would be negligent if we created the impression that selecting a comprehensive approach to classroom management entails only benefits and no costs. Three principal reservations exist: *inflexibility, training,* and *commitment.*

Teachers are professionals, and one of the basic tenets of any profession is that every client should be treated as an individual. Many approaches to classroom management prescribe strategies for dealing with problematic situations rather than individuals. For example, when a student talks out of turn, some approaches fail to take into account whether or not the behavior is chronic. In certain instances, such as when a student rarely speaks in class, talking out of turn may even seem desirable. A teacher's ability to handle each behavioral incident individually may be decreased by adherence to certain comprehensive approaches.

Obtaining training in an approach typically requires time and money. In some cases, the employer picks up the costs of training, but time must be contributed by teachers. Time tends to be the scarcest commodity in any teacher's life. Training in classroom management may necessitate involvement in a college or university course or participation in a series of special workshops. Sometimes, though, teachers are permitted to attend these workshops during "released time" from the classroom, thus reducing the cost of training.

A third possible cost of adopting an approach is less easy to assess than the preceding two. In order for an approach to work well, a teacher must make a serious commitment to using it.

Commitment requires energy. Generally it is less taxing to "play it by ear" and handle classroom management problems as they arise. Some teachers are willing to tolerate a lower level of effectiveness in order to avoid making a commitment to a particular approach.

It is up to each teacher to decide whether or not the benefits of selecting an approach to classroom management outweigh the costs. Such a decision depends a great deal on particular teaching assignments. It is difficult to imagine making this kind of decision apart from an actual classroom context. The nine approaches covered in ᵗhis book are discussed in the contexts of hypothetical but, we hope, realistic elementary and secondary classrooms. We realize, however, that every class is, to some extent, unique. Therefore, you will most likely need to modify our observations to fit your own particular circumstances.

Before we conclude this introductory chapter and proceed to the nine approaches to classroom management, we need to mention a fifth and final assumption underlying our work. We regard teaching as one of the most important, challenging, and frustrating occupations in contemporary society. The importance of teaching is linked directly to our future. Its challenge is to take young people from varying backgrounds and with varying abilities and instill within them the attitudes, knowledge, and skills to pursue their dreams successfully and to contribute to the well-being of society. The frustration of teaching lies in the fact that this demanding responsibility often must be undertaken amidst public criticism, uncertainty, and low levels of financial support.

## Assumption No. 5

*Teaching is one of the most important, challenging, and frustrating occupations in contemporary society.*

Because teachers face so many sources of frustration, we believe that anything that can be done to alleviate even one source promises to contribute to greater job satisfaction and, ultimately, more effective teaching. This book strives to demonstrate that a wealth of resources is available to those interested in developing their classroom management skills and that teachers need not feel they are all alone in their quest to reduce student behavior problems.

# ALTERNATIVE APPROACHES
# TO CLASSROOM
# MANAGEMENT

In this chapter we introduce nine approaches to classroom management. Some derive from research on effective education. Others are based on the clinical experiences of psychologists working with troubled youngsters. One is rooted in organization theory. The approaches include Assertive Discipline, Behavior Modification, Logical Consequences, Positive Peer Culture, Reality Therapy, Social Literacy, Systematic Management Plan for School Discipline, Teacher Effectiveness Training, and Transactional Analysis. Actually, two of the approaches—Positive Peer Culture and Systematic Management Plan for School Discipline—are less designs for how to manage particular classrooms than blueprints for minimizing problems on a schoolwide basis. We included them because we feel some teachers may find it useful to think about student behavior in a schoolwide as well as a classroom context. The nine approaches represent only a few of the more publicized strategies for managing student behavior. It would be impossible to review all of the locally developed programs and research-based prescriptions for effective classroom management.[1] Even some relatively well known approaches such as Equal Opportunity in the Classroom, Instructional Theory Into Practice (ITIP) and TRIBES have been excluded, primarily because of the lack of commercially published descriptive material.

To expect each of the nine approaches to be unique would be a mistake. Many share common features. For example, all blend

---

[1] Readers interested in reading about the variety of programs and research dealing with classroom management are advised to refer to Daniel L. Duke, ed., *Classroom Management* (Chicago: The University of Chicago Press, 1979).

9

elements of problem prevention with techniques for problem intervention. Prevention encompasses activities intended to reduce the likelihood that a certain problem will recur. Intervention, on the other hand, aims at stopping a specific instance of problem behavior. Where differences exist among the nine approaches, they frequently result from different perceptions of the relative importance of prevention and intervention.

We introduce each of the approaches by looking at its goals, origins, general characteristics, the extent to which it has been implemented, the assumptions it makes about how students and teachers behave, the potential problems of actually using it, and the questions which a teacher using the approach might ask herself about how to utilize it. Our intention in this chapter is to provide only an overview of each approach. Specific examples of how the approaches can be applied to particular student behavior problems appear in Part II.

Before proceeding, we should stress the fact that our intention is *not* to serve as spokespersons for any of the approaches to classroom management, including our own. Our role, instead, is that of "consumer's guide," raising awareness of alternatives and pointing out issues in need of consideration. Later, when we give examples of how various approaches can be applied to the resolution of behavior problems, we make *no* pretense that our applications would be endorsed by the authors of the approaches. We place ourselves in the positions of educators making an honest effort to understand the utility of popular approaches to classroom management. Of course, we recognize the fact that individuals, even if they have been thoroughly trained in an approach, are likely to interpret and implement techniques in somewhat idiosyncratic ways. Readers desiring further information or training regarding particular approaches are urged to contact qualified instructors or consult materials provided by developers. A resource guide to assist in this process appears at the end of the book.

## Assertive Discipline

A teacher using Assertive Discipline possesses a clear sense of how students should behave in order for her to accomplish her teaching duties. She does not tolerate attempts by individuals to interfere with her instruction or other students' learning. Students who do not obey class rules receive one warning and then are subjected to a series of increasingly more serious sanctions, culminating in an administrative conference. The teacher refuses to devote time or attention to disruptive students, reserving these resources for those who are conscientious and well behaved.

The goal of Assertive Discipline is to foster in teachers a feeling that they are "in charge" in the classroom. The essence of the approach is captured in the following statement by its author, Lee Canter:

> An assertive teacher will actively respond to a child's inappropriate behavior by clearly communicating to the child her disapproval of the behavior, followed by what she wants the child to do.[2]

## Origins
It is no coincidence that an approach called Assertive Discipline should have appeared in the mid-seventies. Teachers, particularly those in urban areas, increasingly feel beset by disruptive student behavior and powerless to do much about it. The student rights movement, pro-student court decisions, the threat of malpractice lawsuits, unsympathetic administrators and parents, and large numbers of students from unfamiliar cultural backgrounds are only some of the factors cited as contributors to the perceived "crisis" in school discipline.

The developer of Assertive Discipline is a former classroom teacher who was impressed by the possibility of applying the principles of Assertiveness Training to teaching. Canter believes that teachers must learn to assert themselves in order to get their needs met. One basic need is the need to do what one is trained to do—in this case, teach. Disruptive student behavior prevents teachers from teaching.

## Characteristics
Assertive Discipline trains teachers to specify guidelines for student behavior, to develop consequences for disobeying the guidelines, and to communicate them clearly and often. At no time does a teacher permit a student to forget who is in charge of the classroom or that class conduct is governed by certain nonnegotiable rules. Students come to realize that the teacher *expects* them to behave in a certain way in class.

When a student disobeys a class rule, his name is written on the board and he is told what he should be doing. If he continues to

---

[2] Lee Canter (with Marlene Canter), *Assertive Discipline* (Los Angeles: Canter and Associates, Inc., 1979), p. 30.

misbehave, a check is written beside his name, indicating that he must stay after school for fifteen minutes. A second check means a half hour after school. A third check results in a phone call home. Continued misconduct leads to an administrative conference ("severe clause"). In certain cases of serious misconduct, a "severe clause" can be invoked without going through the other steps.

An attractive feature of Assertive Discipline to many teachers is the fact they know there is a clearly established point beyond which they no longer have to try to discipline a student. Once a student receives a "severe clause" or four checks, he is referred to an administrator, freeing the teacher to get on with instruction.

In order for Assertive Discipline to function effectively, Canter stresses, teachers must reinforce appropriate behavior in addition to punishing inappropriate behavior. Teachers are urged to develop "positive consequences" that can be used when students are "on task" and respectful of the rights of others.

## Extent of Use

In-service workshops are the primary vehicle by which Assertive Discipline is offered to teachers.[3] These workshops can be run for interested educators from a given region or exclusively for the faculty of a single school. During a standard two-day workshop, teachers are pushed, entertained, and cajoled into believing that their attitudes determine whether or not they are effective classroom managers. Teachers are helped to develop lists of classroom rules, consequences for rule breaking, and rewards for students who obey rules. As of 1982, Assertive Discipline workshops have been offered primarily on the West Coast, but interest is building elsewhere in the United States. Assertive Discipline promotional literature indicates that 300,000 educators nationwide have been trained in the approach.

## Assumptions

Assertive Discipline is premised on the notion that teacher attitudes influence teacher behavior which, in turn, influences student behavior. If a teacher does not believe he is capable of controlling his class, the likelihood is great that he will act in ways that undermine his control. Failure to communicate expectations of appropriate and inappropriate behavior is one characteristic of such a teacher.

---

3 Those interested in more details about Assertive Discipline should write to Canter and Associates, Inc., P.O. Box 64517, Los Angeles, CA 90064.

Canter divides teachers into three types: nonassertive, hostile, and assertive. Nonassertive teachers allow themselves to be pushed around by students, while hostile teachers harm students by imposing controls in an arbitrary or negative manner. Assertive teachers believe in their abilities and their right to use them to foster student learning. As Canter maintains, such a teacher "says what she means and means what she says."

Because teacher attitudes are the heart of Assertive Discipline, there are few explicit assumptions about student behavior. Canter does seem to feel, however, that students appreciate having limits placed on their behavior and that they respond to sanctions as well as rewards. He also implies that, in the absence of clearly expressed limits, students will try to get away with whatever they can.

## Potential Problems

Assertive Discipline is designed primarily for use in classrooms. Since many of the student behavior problems that most alarm teachers occur outside class, the approach may not offer much help with a significant source of teacher concern.

Within class, the approach may reduce rule breaking but not necessarily without negative by-products. Assertive Discipline provides no opportunities for students to learn or practice conflict-resolution skills. Rather than learning to be responsible, students remain dependent on the teacher to intervene and handle behavior problems.

A third potential problem with Assertive Discipline is the fact that, if poorly implemented, it can create an uncomfortable and possibly repelling environment. In theory, of course, teachers are supposed to devote time to reinforcing appropriate behavior as well as sanctioning inappropriate behavior. In practice, though, teachers sometimes stress sanctions to the exclusion of reinforcements, thus creating a negative classroom climate. A repressive classroom can foster increased acting out by students when they leave the class.

## Key Questions

*Teachers who employ Assertive Discipline tend to ask themselves the following kinds of questions:*

*1. Does the problem behavior violate a classroom rule?*

2. *If so, what is the punishment for disobeying the rule?*
3. *Have this rule and punishment been communicated to the student?*
4. *Is this rule infraction so serious that it qualifies as an immediate "severe clause"?*
5. *Do I have positive reinforcers established for students who behave appropriately?*
6. *Am I willing to assert myself and enforce the rule already established, or will I ignore this behavior?*

# Behavior Modification

Perhaps the best known of all systematic approaches to dealing with behavior problems, Behavior Modification encompasses a variety of techniques, ranging from simple rewards to elaborate peer reinforcement schemes. The common thread running through all Behavior Modification techniques is the belief that behavior is shaped by environmental factors. The primary goal of Behavior Modification is *changing* behavior. Unlike psychotherapeutic approaches, it places relatively little emphasis on understanding the root causes of the behaviors to be changed.

A teacher using Behavior Modification does not spend a lot of time trying to understand the reasons why a particular student fails to obey class rules. She analyzes what occurs immediately before and after acts of disobedience. This knowledge allows her to modify the situation so that factors that set the stage for behavior problems or that reinforce them once they take place can be controlled. The teacher strives to provide reinforcement — perhaps in the form of praise or tokens redeemable for privileges — only when the student behaves appropriately.

## Origins

Behavior Modification derives from the work of behavioral psychologists, including Ivan Pavlov's experiments with conditioned reflexes and John B. Watson's development of Behavior Therapy. The principal contemporary exponent of the approach is B. F. Skinner. Skinner maintains that it is irresponsible not to use scientific control to shape human behavior. He has been a major influence behind the adaptation of clinical Behavior Modification techniques to classroom settings.

## Characteristics

When inappropriate behavior occurs, advocates of Behavior Modification tend to look for methods of altering the immediate environment in such a way as to reduce the likelihood that the behavior will recur. Alterations may involve such activities as providing greater reinforcement when appropriate behavior takes place, ignoring inappropriate behavior, and introducing unpleasant (aversive) consequences when inappropriate behavior occurs. The expectation underlying Behavior Modification is that such activities can be gradually diminished over time as the inappropriate behavior becomes less frequent. Behavior modifiers do not believe that behavior problems can be eliminated overnight through the simple imposition of a rule or a punishment. Not all behavior problems entail actual behavior. Some involve the absence of behavior—for example, the student who fails to turn work in on time. Behavior Modification is designed to elicit appropriate behavior as well as reduce the frequency of inappropriate behavior. To accomplish the former objective, it may be necessary to reinforce any approximation to the desired behavior. The process may involve weeks or even months.

## Extent of Use

Probably more training and research has focused on Behavior Modification than any other classroom management approach. Elementary teachers, counselors, and educators working with handicapped students have used it extensively. Most schools of education boast at least one educational psychologist specializing in Behavior Modification, and some possess entire departments of such individuals. An assortment of books on Behavior Modification has been published for educators.[4]　　(

## Assumptions

Behavior Modification assumes that behavior is learned and that it is learned as a result of reinforcement. Reinforcement generally is perceived to originate in the environment rather than within the individual. For this reason, Behavior Modification sometimes has been criticized for ignoring the influence of free will and internal motivation.

---

4 Some books that may be useful to classroom teachers include Harvey F. Clarizio, *Toward Positive Classroom Discipline*, 2d ed. (New York: John Wiley & Sons, 1976) and Howard N. Sloane, *Classroom Management* (New York: John Wiley & Sons, 1976).

The above assumption leads to the conclusion that inappropriate student behavior occurs because the consequences of the behavior are reinforcing. To reduce the behavior, a teacher must identify these consequences and alter them. Thus, if a student frequently interrupts a lecture because the teacher too easily gets sidetracked, it may be necessary for the teacher to work on keeping her remarks focused, thus eliminating the satisfaction the student receives from diverting the course of the lecture.

The same assumption underlying student behavior characterizes teacher behavior. Thus, teachers who utilize Behavior Modification may need to consider their own behavior and how it may be subject to reinforcement from the classroom environment. Anyone who has spent time working with students knows that they play a powerful role as reinforcers of teacher behavior. The teacher, for example, who stops assigning homework because few students turn it in on time has had her behavior effectively modified. Understanding the nature of student reinforcement can lead teachers to improve their classroom management skills.

## Potential Problems

Because Behavior Modification is more concerned with changing inappropriate behavior than understanding its origins, teachers who use the approach may sometimes overlook important elements in a student's history. Lack of awareness of the possible relationship between student background and present behavior can detract from the effectiveness of teacher-student communications and leave the student feeling somewhat adrift in an impersonal environment.

Behavior Modification proponents frequently attribute student misconduct to attention seeking. This oversimplified explanation ignores the contribution to acting out made by such additional factors as a desire for revenge and a need for power. More will be said about these factors in the following discussion of Rudolf Dreikurs' work.

A final problem concerning Behavior Modification is the difficulty of locating adequate reinforcers for older students. While candy, praise, and tokens may work well in elementary school, they often fail to motivate high school students.

## Key Questions

*Essential to developing Behavior Modification techniques is careful systematic observation of behavior and analysis of its consequences. The questions a teacher should ask focus less*

*on the root causes of behavior problems than on character-*
*istics of the behavior itself. As a result, questions generally*
*do not begin with "why."*

1. *What is the specific behavior that requires modifica-*
   *tion (elimination, reduction, increase)?*
2. *When does the behavior occur?*
3. *What are the immediate consequences of this behav-*
   *ior? In other words, what occurs in the classroom*
   *when a student manifests this behavior?*
4. *How can these consequences serve to reinforce the in-*
   *appropriate behavior?*
5. *How can the consequences be altered?*
6. *How can appropriate behavior be reinforced in the*
   *future?*

# Logical Consequences

"Logical Consequences" refers to a major component of a comprehensive approach to dealing with young people, both in school
and at home. The essence of the approach is the encouragement
of responsible behavior. Rudolf Dreikurs, the originator of the
Logical Consequences approach, has said,[5]

> We can no longer run schools for the children; we have to take them
> in as partners, win their support. This cannot be done without intro-
> ducing democratic approaches in each class.

A teacher using the ideas of Dreikurs involves students in the
development of class rules. He also takes care to make certain that
the consequences of disobeying a rule are logical outgrowths of
the misconduct. It would be illogical, for example, to use extra
homework as a consequence for failure to complete assignments
because it is important for students to regard homework as helpful rather than punitive. A logical consequence of failure to complete homework is for the student to spend all free time in class
completing assignments while his fellow students choose to do
what they wish.

---

[5] Rudolf Dreikurs, Bernice Grunwald, and Floy C. Pepper, *Maintaining Sanity in
the Classroom: Illustrated Teaching Techniques* (New York: Harper & Row,
1971), p. 172.

## Origins

A follower of Alfred Adler, Viennese psychiatrist Dreikurs emigrated to the United States in 1937. He subsequently established two Adlerian institutes in Chicago and began applying his mentor's precepts to the tasks of parenting and classroom management. Among the results of these efforts are a training program for educators and three education-related books: *Psychology in the Classroom* (1968), *Maintaining Sanity in the Classroom* (1971), and *Discipline Without Tears* (1972).

## Characteristics

The basis for teaching students to be responsible is making them aware of their behavior and its impact on others and giving them an opportunity to help determine how to correct the situation. Awareness is developed in teacher-student conferences, which follow instances of inappropriate behavior. The teacher tries to help the student understand why he has behaved in a certain way and to involve the student in identifying the consequences of his behavior. In order to be "logical" or natural, these consequences should be directly related to the problem behavior. Thus, if a student defaces school property, he might be encouraged to repair the damage. A key dimension of Logical Consequences involves allowing the student to participate in the disciplinary process. All too often, Dreikurs contends, teachers set themselves up as the sole determiners of corrective courses of action, a process that denies students any responsible role in classroom management.

Not all interactions are on a teacher-to-student basis. On occasions when an entire class is unsettled, it may be appropriate to engage everyone in a group discussion of the problem behavior and its consequences. Dreikurs also urges teachers to involve students in generating classroom rules and procedures.

## Extent of Use

Dreikurs' approach has been offered to educators, youth workers, and parents in thousands of local workshops over the past decade. A network of local trainers is responsible for running these sessions and for providing follow-up technical support.

## Assumptions

Two basic assumptions underlie Dreikurs' approach: (1) student behavior is goal-directed and (2) people learn best through concrete experiences.

Dreikurs argues that student misbehavior can be traced to at least one of the following four goals: (1) attention getting, (2) power, (3) revenge, or (4) display of inadequacy. The key to correcting the behavior problem lies in making the student aware of which of these goals is prompting his conduct. The corrective strategy for dealing with the behavior problem will vary somewhat depending on the student's goal.

The Logical Consequences approach embraces the old maxim that experience is the best teacher. Students are more likely to learn to behave responsibly if they are given opportunities to exercise responsibility. Dreikurs thus calls on teachers to engage students in correcting their own behavior and in making classroom rules.

As for teacher behavior, Dreikurs assumes that the best classroom manager is the teacher who possesses the psychological skills and understanding needed to diagnose student behavior problems and communicate this information to students. No matter how capable a teacher is when it comes to detecting the reasons why a student misbehaves, if she cannot communicate with him, it is doubtful that the problem can be resolved. Teachers must be able to discuss the goals of student behavior without conveying a sense that the student is bad or a failure. They also need to encourage rather than praise (encouragement, unlike praise, makes no statement about the worth of the student). Finally, teachers should interact with students in such a way as to provide ideas and direction without establishing dominance or building up dependence.

## Potential Problems

A great deal of the success of Dreikurs' ideas in classrooms depends on how correctly teachers diagnose the motives underlying student misconduct. Incorrect diagnoses may undermine student confidence in the teacher and make subsequent interactions more difficult.

A second potential problem involves the amount of time required to implement the various aspects of Dreikurs' approach. Individual conferences with students can require considerable time, as do class meetings designed to develop rules and consequences for disobedience. Unless a teacher regards classroom management as an integral part of being an effective teacher, it is likely that this investment of time will be greeted with resentment.

Identifying and implementing "logical" consequences poses a third potential difficulty. For example, what is a logical conse-

quence of a victimless act of disobedience, such as smoking a ciga-
rette? Do teachers have the right to confiscate personal property
— such as skateboards and radios — if it can create a nuisance?
What consequences can be legally imposed by school authorities
when one student physically abuses another?

---

### Key Questions

*Teachers who employ the ideas of Dreikurs may find
themselves asking the following questions:*

1. *What is the goal of this student's inappropriate
   behavior?*
2. *When is a good time to talk with this student about
   his behavior?*
3. *What are the logical consequences of the student's
   behavior and how can I make the student aware of
   these consequences?*
4. *How can I avoid dictating a corrective procedure to
   the student and encourage the student to propose his
   own solution?*

---

## Positive Peer Culture

Positive Peer Culture, as the title suggests, is an all-inclusive approach to dealing with young people.[6] The heart of the program
is the belief that adults who work with youth, particularly troubled
youth, typically monopolize the giving of help. Originators Harry
H. Vorrath and Larry K. Brendtro offer a variety of ways to re-
structure environments in which young people live and study so
that they can assume some responsibility for helping themselves.
Unlike approaches that ask whether an individual wants to receive
assistance, Positive Peer Culture asks if he wants to provide help.

A teacher using Positive Peer Culture does not try to resolve all
student problems that arise in class. She creates opportunities for
troubled youngsters to help each other. In group problem-solving
sessions she serves as a facilitator rather than a clinician or instruc-

---

6 Harry H. Vorrath and Larry K. Brendtro, *Positive Peer Culture* (Chicago: Aldine
Publishing Company, 1974).

tor. It is important for her to remember that problems are a normal part of growing up.

## Origins

First developed in a New Jersey residential treatment program for delinquent youth, Positive Peer Culture has been expanded and modified since the late 1950s. Vorrath attempted to adapt the peer-oriented treatment model to other settings, including schools. Positive Peer Culture received national attention when Howard James, a Pulitzer Prize-winning journalist, wrote a book describing successful programs for problem youth. *Children in Trouble: A National Scandal* (New York: Pocket Books, 1971) detailed Vorrath's intervention at a reform school in Minnesota where young persons had rioted and fled. James wrote, "I was more heartened by what I saw at Red Wing (Minnesota) than by anything else going on in large institutions anywhere in America" (p. 126).

## Characteristics

Working in single-sex groups of nine with an adult leader, young people learn how to identify personal and group problems and work toward their solution. Unlike confrontation groups seeking similar objectives, however, Positive Peer Culture groups work on offering as safe an environment as possible for members. In time, as others bring concerns before the group, reluctant members begin to open up about their own feelings. Eventually they are able to tell their life stories to the group, affording other members a chance to see how they view themselves. In this way the group can start to provide the kind of support that each member requires to work through his or her own problems.

Positive Peer Culture is essentially a set of guidelines for running effective groups. Those who receive training learn how to detect group power structure and stages of group development and how to function as group leaders. Meetings generally center on individual reporting of problems and brainstorming ways in which the group can help overcome them.

## Extent of Use

Positive Peer Culture is detailed in the book by the same name published in 1974 (see Footnote 5). It is widely read by juvenile justice personnel and youth services workers, but educators are less familiar with it. While no figures are available on the extent of its use, Vorrath and Brendtro report that the approach is operating in all parts of the country and in a variety of settings. It appears that educational programs designed specifically for troubled youth would be most inclined to adopt Positive Peer Culture. Such programs include reform schools and alternative schools for students who cannot function in conventional settings. The state of Indiana recently has contracted with Positive Peer Culture to renovate its residential facility for troubled girls. Renovation projects have been completed in fourteen other states.

## Assumptions

Positive Peer Culture assumes that problems are normal. Rather than focusing on the elimination of problems—an unrealistic goal at best and an undesirable one at worst—the approach encourages individuals to view problems as opportunities. In the case of Positive Peer Culture, youth problems provide opportunities for peers to learn how to help each other. Such opportunities generally have been lacking in elementary and secondary schools.

The preceding comment suggests a second assumption: the peer group can be a positive force in the lives of young people. Too often educators operate under the opposite assumption, namely that the peer group always works to undermine adult authority and encourage misconduct. Vorrath and Brendtro counter this conventional belief with many examples of situations in which peer groups reinforce caring and responsibility. They imply that adults get from youth exactly what they expect. If they expect disruption, they will tend to get disruption. If they expect cooperation, they will tend to get cooperation.

Positive Peer Culture encompasses a number of assumptions about individual behavior that also challenge conventional beliefs. For instance, it maintains that a person need not overcome all of his own problems in order to help solve the problems of others. Also, individuals are assumed to be willing to help others for the sake of helping. Rewards or inducements are not considered a necessary component of Positive Peer Culture.

Unlike some of the other approaches described in this book, Positive Peer Culture makes few assumptions about adult behavior. The key to the approach lies in giving young people opportunities to develop and demonstrate skill in helping each other. The main way in which the adult group leader can contribute is to function as a model of helpful, caring behavior.

## Potential Problems

Teachers who decide to establish Positive Peer Culture problem-solving groups in their classrooms will find that considerable time is required. To be effective the groups need to meet regularly. Since the groups should be made up of no more than nine students of the same sex, using class time for group meetings usually entails making arrangements for supervision of nonparticipating students.

Positive Peer Culture is not an approach suited to on-the-spot intervention. Other strategies must be used to handle emergencies when they arise. Eventually, however, the problems leading to such incidents may be dealt with in the groups.

A final concern with Positive Peer Culture is the need for a long-term commitment from teachers who agree to serve as group leaders. The approach should not be adopted for a brief period and then abandoned. The effectiveness of Positive Peer Culture lies, in part, in the continued presence of settings in which troubled youth can express their problems.

---

### Key Questions

*Teachers who are thinking about utilizing Positive Peer Culture in their classrooms must realize that they may not be able to offer as comprehensive an application of the approach as can be provided in a residential treatment center. Still, there seem to be various ways in which the approach can be used. Relevant questions to consider include the following:*

1. *What are my expectations regarding how students relate to each other?*
2. *Can I begin to regard student problems as opportunities to help students learn responsibility and caring?*
3. *Can I find time to operate peer meetings or can I encourage others in the school to make these opportunities available?*
4. *Are there ways in which I can encourage students to help each other instead of relying on me or another adult?*

---

## Reality Therapy

In his best-seller *Schools Without Failure* William Glasser attempts to apply to schools and classrooms many of the clinical insights he originally discussed in *Reality Therapy*.[7] His primary goal, as is also true for Logical Consequences and Positive Peer Culture, is to develop responsible behavior among young people. The techniques he recommends and the assumptions underlying them, however, differ.

A teacher using Reality Therapy tries to provide opportunities for students to become aware of why things sometimes go wrong for them in school. One such opportunity may be a regular class discussion group. When a student is involved in breaking a rule or failing to complete an assignment, the teacher sees that he makes a formal commitment to correct his behavior. Because Reality Therapy holds that student behavior problems often derive from low self-esteem, teachers who adopt the approach need to eliminate situations where students are likely to experience failure.

## Origins

A psychiatrist by training, Glasser spent eleven years working at a residential treatment center for California's most delinquent girls. In the 1960s he became concerned about the plight of minority students as he read accounts of the low quality of education in inner-city schools. *Schools Without Failure* contains many suggestions for creating learning environments where young people, particularly those who have experienced negative feelings about schools, can take an active interest in self-improvement.

## Characteristics

Glasser's approach begins with self-awareness. Teachers utilizing his ideas help troubled students become aware of their problems. Once the awareness exists and an understanding of the presumed origins of the problems has been gained, students are asked to commit to a course of corrective action. Teachers serve as resources to assist students in fulfilling their commitments. In instances where students fail to follow through on their commitments, they are required to deal with the consequences. Teachers are warned not to permit students to abandon their commitments without considering the implications of such actions.

Glasser tends to view interactions between individual teachers and students as the key to more effective classroom management, but he does not ignore broader organizational concerns. Among

---

[7] William Glasser, *Schools Without Failure* (New York: Harper & Row, 1969); William Glasser, *Reality Therapy* (New York: Harper & Row, 1965).

other changes in the way schools are operated, he calls for the elimination of graded report cards, increased time for groups of teachers to meet to discuss students who are beginning to experience difficulties, and student involvement in making rules. If students have to be referred to "the office," Glasser recommends they be instructed to write a plan for changing their behavior. Reality Therapy, like Positive Peer Culture, also makes extensive use of class meetings as opportunities for students to develop skills in expressing their problems publicly and exploring solutions on a group basis.

## Extent of Use

Glasser's book has sold well for more than a decade, and he has been a popular speaker across the United States. His numerous workshops tend to attract elementary teachers, who find his suggestions for daily class meetings helpful. Little has been written about applications of his techniques at the secondary level.

## Assumptions

Glasser writes primarily about student academic problems. He makes the important assumption, verified by research, that student behavior problems often result from academic problems, however. The failing student, frustrated by his inability to function at the teacher's level of expectations, frequently expresses his uneasiness by disobeying class rules.

To correct an academic problem, Glasser believes, a student must make a specific commitment to overcome the problem. To make such a commitment presupposes that the student is aware of the nature of his or her academic problem. Often this is not the case. Teachers who confront troubled students may take for granted that students clearly understand the source of their poor performance when, in fact, students do not possess such understanding. A student, therefore, may attribute his low grades to poor teaching, while his teacher lays the blame on inadequate motivation.

Glasser believes that the real problem may be linked to the belief — held by many students, he claims — that they have little chance of achieving success in school or in life. Failure in school serves to confirm student cynicism and low self-esteem. Loneliness and lack of love often lie at the heart of such negative feelings. To correct the situation, Glasser urges teachers to provide more opportunities for all students to be successful. These opportunities range from student involvement in school activities to academic tasks that are designed to build on what students already know.

Glasser makes several assumptions regarding teacher, as well as student, behavior. For example, he believes teachers too often *expect* a certain proportion of their students to fail. In addition, they frequently "give up" on students with behavior problems before they have determined if these problems derive from correctable academic deficiencies. Glasser also claims teachers assume too often that students are motivated to benefit from instruction. He feels motivation is no different from reading or calculating—it must be learned.

## Potential Problems

As in the case of Positive Peer Culture, Reality Therapy requires considerable time to implement. To be effective, group discussions should be scheduled on a regular basis. When students make a commitment to work on a problem, teachers must be prepared to monitor their progress. The nature of these time demands may explain why more elementary teachers utilize the approach than secondary teachers.

Another potential problem with Reality Therapy concerns the idea of eliminating situations where students are likely to fail. No one can succeed all the time in real life. Learning to deal effectively with failure may be as important an educational objective as learning to achieve what one sets out to do. Glasser is vague about when teachers should and should not allow students to fail.

---

## Key Questions

*Any approach that considers problem awareness to be a first step toward student improvement may be expected to stress teacher awareness as a critical element in the process of classroom management. Teachers interested in Glasser's approach may ask themselves the following questions:*

1. *Does this problem behavior (by student X) relate to the student's academic history?*
2. *Does the student possess skills and/or resources necessary to perform adequately in class?*
3. *Does the student understand the nature of the problem?*
4. *Is the student willing to make a commitment to correct the problem?*

# Social Literacy Training

One of the most recent approaches to classroom management, Social Literacy Training encompasses an assortment of activities designed to foster more open, honest interactions between teachers and students.[8] Alfred Alschuler, developer of Social Literacy Training, believes that many interpersonal relationships in schools are characterized by oppression. To correct the situation, he urges teachers and students to engage in dialogue, speak "true words about central conflicts," and develop "critical consciousness."

A teacher using Social Literacy Training tends to regard acts of misconduct as symptoms of more fundamental problems. Her goal is to foster open communications with students about these problems. In the event that students are misbehaving and upset because of school-based circumstances, the teacher engages in various conflict-resolution exercises with students. The objective of these activities is to develop "no-lose" solutions—in other words, solutions that do not help students at the teacher's expense or vice versa.

## Origins

Social Literacy Training derives from the work of the great Brazilian educator, Paulo Freire. Alschuler worked for a while as a clinical psychologist in Ecuador and became familiar with the philosophy underlying Freire's approach to adult literacy training. Freire bases his work on the belief that people must develop the ability to create their world, a world in which it is easier to love. Alschuler returned to the United States and adapted Freire's technique to classroom and school contexts. In his work he strives to discourage teachers and students from blaming each other for their problems and to help them learn to cooperate in problem resolution.

## Characteristics

Social Literacy Training involves a series of consciousness-raising activities designed to provide instruction in problem solving and to foster dialogue and cooperation among teachers and students. For example, the "nuclear problem-solving process" calls on participants to (1) collaboratively name patterns of conflict in school or classroom, (2) analyze the rules and roles of the system that

---

[8] Alfred S. Alschuler, *School Discipline: A Socially Literate Solution* (New York: McGraw-Hill Book Company, 1980).

contribute to this conflict, and (3) democratically negotiate solutions. Another activity is the Discipline Game, designed to develop skill in creating alternatives to punishment by asking players to look at troublesome situations from different perspectives. Thus, students may be called upon to look at cutting class through the eyes of a teacher, while teachers are asked to see the same problem as a student would see it. A third activity entails the identification of "central conflicts." Teachers and students spend several hours naming the important words they use in school, prioritizing the list of words, and zeroing in on those that describe basic conflicts. All of these training activities require active student involvement, indicating Alschuler's belief that effective classroom management is a joint enterprise.

## Extent of Use

Social Literacy Training first appeared in an article by Alschuler in 1974. Between that time and the publication in 1980 of *School Discipline: A Socially Literate Solution*, the training has been offered in over a hundred workshops across the United States. Alschuler and his colleagues at the University of Massachusetts have personally supervised the implementation of the approach in two school systems — Springfield, Massachusetts, and Hartford, Connecticut. Social Literacy Training was credited by the author with reducing much of the tension in these two systems, tension that arose in part from school integration efforts. Alschuler also has served as consultant to other school systems facing integration problems.

## Assumptions

The basic assumption underlying Social Literacy Training is that classroom problems can be resolved without either students or teacher "losing." In order to achieve "no-lose" solutions, however, teachers and students must develop the ability to communicate openly, honestly, and frequently. In most schools, Alschuler believes, few opportunities for such interaction exist. His activities are designed to increase opportunities for productive dialogue.

A second assumption is that conflicts and problems are a natural part of human interaction. To enable teachers and students to function effectively, they need to learn how to resolve these conflicts and problems. Alschuler does not believe that individuals are born with this capacity. Teachers who subscribe to the Social Literacy Training approach take a broad enough view of the curriculum to permit students to work on conflict resolution and problem solving in a regular classroom context.

## Potential Problems

Social Literacy Training requires considerable time and coordination. Like Positive Peer Culture, it is unsuited to dealing with emergencies in an expedient fashion. The activities and games must be planned and followed up. Teachers who regard any departure from academic subject matter as a waste of time are likely to feel uncomfortable devoting energy to fostering open communications and identifying personal and interpersonal conflicts.

Another potential problem is that some students may misinterpret the gamelike nature of many Social Literacy exercises and not take them seriously. In such instances, the exercises conceivably could contribute to increased levels of tension and misconduct.

---

### Key Questions

*The questions below are intended to be asked by both teachers and students. They concern the identification of areas where problems consistently arise and possible ways of resolving the problems.*

1. *What is the problem?*
2. *Is the problem located in individuals or in rules and roles?*
3. *Have any changes in classroom or school organization been considered?*
4. *Is the problem-solving process democratic?*
5. *Is the solution mutually agreeable and satisfying?*

---

## Systematic Management Plan for School Discipline (SMPSD)

Although originally developed as an approach to schoolwide reorganization, the Systematic Management Plan for School Discipline (SMPSD) offers valuable suggestions to teachers concerned about classroom behavior problems.[9] Rather than focusing on ways to modify instructional techniques or personal interactions, the SMPSD deals with changes in the organizational structure of schools. These changes are intended to increase the likeli-

---

9 Daniel L. Duke and Adrienne M. Meckel, *Managing Student Behavior Problems* (New York: Teachers College Press, 1980).

hood that behavior problems can be managed with minimal interference in the normal instructional routine.

A single teacher cannot implement the SMPSD alone. Rather, it must be utilized by a group of teachers in concert with the school administration. These individuals reorganize their school along lines that permit rules to be developed collaboratively, problems to be monitored by teams of educators, and consequences for disobeying rules to be made uniform. The SMPSD requires students with problems to be followed up on a regular basis by all the teachers with whom they come in contact. Teachers are discouraged from allowing themselves to become isolated from their colleagues when disciplinary problems arise.

## Origins

The SMPSD first appeared in 1976 as a series of recommendations for secondary school administrators confronting chronic behavior problems. The recommendations were derived from organization theory and existing practices identified by educators as effective. By the time *Managing Student Behavior Problems* appeared in 1980, the SMPSD had been adjusted to include ideas for teachers interested in developing a more systematic approach to classroom management.

## Characteristics

The SMPSD is divided into seven components, dealing with the following activities:

1. Understanding the school as a rule-governed organization.
2. Collecting the data necessary for understanding and improving school discipline.
3. Expanding the school's conflict-resolution capacity.
4. Developing a team approach to discipline problems.
5. Involving parents in school discipline.
6. Providing reinforcing environments for learning.
7. Providing professional development opportunities for faculty and staff.

The overall approach is a collaborative one. Teachers are encouraged to work closely with colleagues, administrators, support staff, parents, and students, rather than trying to "go it alone." It does little good for one teacher to get his own classroom under control if the rest of the school is disorganized. Working with others to generate rules and consequences, identify students beginning to have problems, and plan strategies to help these students increases the likelihood that school discipline will be consistent and effective.

The SMPSD does not encompass a single technique or set of skills. Rather, it offers a variety of ideas for handling problems already in existence as well as preventing certain problems from occurring in the first place. Teachers are urged to consider the value of reducing classroom rules to the bare minimum, enforcing these rules consistently, and testing students on their knowledge of rules and consequences. Instructions are provided on how to collect and disseminate useful data on student behavior, run an effective troubleshooting meeting, and set up in-school alternative programs for troubled students.

## Extent of Use

The SMPSD has served as the basis for workshops and organizational development activities in numerous school districts, especially in New York and California. It has proven particularly useful for educators working in large urban schools. Most schools do not find it necessary to adopt all fifty-five recommendations, however. The SMPSD is premised on the belief that the needs of schools vary from one location to the next.

## Assumptions

The SMPSD is based on the assumption that how individuals behave in schools is related to how schools are organized. If students misbehave frequently, they may be communicating their discomfort with certain aspects of school organization. Rather than trying to change student behavior directly, the SMPSD begins by attempting to change school organization. The assumption supporting this strategy is that schools are intended to serve students, not vice versa.

Several other key assumptions underlie the SMPSD. First, it is assumed that student behavior problems never can be totally eliminated. Instead of striving in vain to prevent such problems, the SMPSD seeks to equip educators with strategies for managing problems so they do not get out of control.

Another assumption is that approaches to improving school discipline that are limited to modifications in classroom management are generally inadequate. What is needed is comprehensive, rather than piecemeal, improvement. The history of efforts to reduce student behavior problems is marked by numerous failures of good ideas naively implemented. For example, training teachers to enforce classroom rules more consistently does little good if different teachers have vastly different rules or if administrators and counselors continue to handle student referrals inconsistently. Effective strategies to reduce behavior problems should not ignore the organizational characteristics of the school.

## Potential Problems

To be effectively implemented, the SMPSD requires planning time, administrative support, and the cooperation of a majority of the teachers in a school. For various reasons, these needs may be difficult to satisfy. For one thing, the inertial forces in many schools are substantial. Teachers are used to dealing with student behavior problems themselves. Asking teachers to see discipline as a schoolwide concern that must be handled on a collaborative basis frequently meets with initial resistance.

Another potential problem concerns additional resources. During an era when school budgets are shrinking, it may be hard to secure the funds necessary to train staff members, coordinate the collection and dissemination of disciplinary data, and contract out services to community agencies. Without such funds, a school's capacity for reorganization may be severely limited.

## Key Questions

*The questions a teacher or, preferably, a group of teachers interested in the SMPSD should ask focus on the possible relationships between behavior problems and school organization.*

1. *Does the problem occur frequently?*
2. *If the problem is chronic, under what circumstances does it occur?*
3. *Are there any characteristics of classroom or school organization (such as how rules or consequences are decided, how conflicts are resolved, etc.) that might contribute to the problem?*
4. *In what ways can the problem be addressed on a comprehensive, schoolwide basis (involving teachers, students, parents, etc.)?*

# Teacher Effectiveness Training (TET)

Thomas Gordon, the originator of Teacher Effectiveness Training (TET), strives to instruct educators in how to reduce negative behavior by clearer, less provocative classroom communication.[10] This goal bespeaks Gordon's belief that it is unproductive to try to force, bribe, cajole, or threaten anyone—students included—in order to accomplish a goal. Dialogue between people is regarded as the course of action most likely to produce effective behavior.

When behavior problems arise, a teacher employing Teacher Effectiveness Training uses them as opportunities to find out what is bothering students. She avoids talking to students in ways that place them on the defensive. Instead, she explains why particular behaviors cause problems for her. Together teacher and student explore ideas for resolving problems so that no one "loses."

## Origins

Gordon, a clinical psychologist trained at the University of Chicago, directed his first efforts at improving relations between parents and students. Following the development of Parent Effectiveness Training, there came a variety of related programs, including TET and Leader Effectiveness Training. All share a common emphasis on the quality of communications between individuals usually regarded as being "in control" and those subject to their control.

## Characteristics

Gordon attempts to operationalize—or put into terms that encompass specific behaviors—relatively abstract educational goals such as "respect for the needs of students" and "democracy in the classroom." He gives meaning to these goals by contrasting how teachers tend to talk to students with alternative means of expression.

For example, teachers frequently put students on the defensive by beginning a statement of concern or irritation with the pronoun "you." Gordon suggests that a less provocative way to convey the same basic sentiment is to use the pronoun "I."

The heart of TET is what Gordon calls Method III, or "no-lose problem resolution"—a series of tactics for handling conflicts be-

---

10 Thomas Gordon, *T.E.T.: Teacher Effectiveness Training* (New York: Peter H. Wyden, Publisher, 1974). Information on workshops can be obtained by writing to the Effectiveness Training Association, 531 Stevens Avenue, Solano Beach, CA 92075.

tween teachers and students when there are no basic value differences. In cases where a teacher and student cannot reach agreement that a problem exists, other tactics are provided.

The six steps of Method III constitute a form of negotiation where teacher and student contribute relatively equally. The process begins with a determination of the problem and who "owns" it. When a student talks with a friend while the teacher is giving directions, the conversation is the teacher's problem if she loses her concentration and gets sidetracked. It is the student's problem if he fails to hear directions that are crucial to completing the assignment.

Possible solutions to the problem then are generated, with teacher and student presenting the same number of ideas. These ideas are evaluated in step three, and any ones that are completely unacceptable to at least one person are rejected. Step four involves deciding on the best remaining solution, which then is followed by the determination of how to implement it. The final step entails assessing how well the proposed solution actually works. Generally, punishments are not considered viable solutions, since they imply that someone (the students) must lose.

When Method III cannot be used because of a failure to agree that a problem exists, teachers may have to settle for modeling their values (in the hopes that the problem will be resolved) or changing their own expectations. In some cases teachers may even "hire" themselves out to students as values consultants and work on student concerns collaboratively.

## Extent of Use

Now in its second printing, *Teacher Effectiveness Training* has served as the basis for training over 42,000 educators. Training originally consisted of a 30-hour program run by one of the approximately 5,000 professionals who make up Effectiveness Training Associates, the organization that oversees all of the effectiveness training programs. Today this program is found primarily on college campuses, where students can earn credit for successfully completing training. Recently, a second version of the training has been developed. Entitled Teacher Effectiveness (TE), it involves more experience-based learning and role-playing and is taught in 30 to 36-hour programs.

## Assumptions

Like the SMPSD, TET is based on the assumption that conflicts between teachers and students will never be totally eliminated.

This basic assumption gives rise to a variety of beliefs concerning how to minimize the impact of conflicts.

The key to effective teaching is perceived to be the relationship between teacher and student. Gordon expects the teacher to take major responsibility for determining the nature of this relationship. As indicated earlier, communication is regarded as the basis for a productive relationship. Therefore TET is devoted to teaching teachers how to talk *with* (as opposed to talk *to*) and listen to students. Gordon does not believe that sanctions or rewards enhance teacher-student relations, a conviction that places him somewhat at odds with advocates of Assertive Discipline and Behavior Modification.

TET also embodies a set of assumptions about how schools encourage behavior problems. For instance, students may not develop responsible habits because teachers tend to step in and resolve conflicts without enlisting student contributions. Other factors which tend to foster problems include the absence of clear-cut rules and the implementation of rules which students have not shared in developing.

## Potential Problems

As in the case of other approaches that rely on direct communication concerning problems, TET can demand considerable time, at least initially. Students generally are unaccustomed to resolving problems through negotiations with teachers. They thus may test the problem-resolution process to see if teachers are bargaining in good faith. Teachers employing TET strategies must be patient as students adjust to the fact that they have a role to play in classroom management.

Some teachers may be unable to accept the TET assumption that force never works. Others may be unwilling to modify their own values when confronted with certain behaviors which students themselves do not regard as problematic. Teachers who lack confidence in themselves or who distrust students may find TET too threatening, since it devolves on students more responsibility than is found in conventional classrooms.

## Key Questions

*The questions which a teacher using TET may ask focus on determining the nature of the problem at hand and how to talk about it with students.*

1. *What is the problem and who "owns" it?*
2. *Is there agreement on the part of all concerned that a problem exists?*
3. *What is the nature of communications between the student(s) involved and me?*
4. *How can the problem be resolved in such a way as to strengthen my relationship with the student(s)?*

# Transactional Analysis (TA)

Like TET, the primary concern of Transactional Analysis (TA) is the nature of communications between people.[11] Communications include both verbal and nonverbal messages and listening as well as speaking. It is the gamelike (implying winning and losing) nature of these communications that most interests exponents of TA.

A teacher using TA tries to diagnose what students are really trying to say when they misbehave. Sometimes diagnostic remarks are shared with the whole class, but usually the teacher waits until she can speak with troubled students alone. TA requires the teacher to function as a clinician, listening carefully to how students perceive their behavior and helping them to understand why it may be inappropriate.

## Origins

Psychoanalyst Eric Berne developed TA in the 1950s in an effort to explain complex psychological concepts in simple language. Originally described in *A Layman's Guide to Psychiatry and Psychoanalysis*, Berne's system did not achieve popular acclaim until the appearance seven years later of his best seller *Games People Play*. Since that time TA principles have been applied to a variety of situations, including the interactions of teachers and students.

## Characteristics

As applied to schools, TA focuses on teachers and their ability to detect when students are playing "games." When teachers are unaware of the gamelike nature of interactions with students, they often behave ineffectively, acting more like parents (tyrants or martyrs) or children (self-centered, complaining) than adults.

Teachers faced with behavior problems are encouraged to meet privately with students. During these sessions teachers explain the behavior they have observed and how it interferes with school-

---

11  Eric Berne, *Games People Play* (New York: Grove Press, 1964).

work and teacher-student relations. The teacher's role in preventing behavior problems also is discussed. Once students achieve some insight into their behavior and begin to share what is bothering them, teachers can shift their role to that of the active listener. Conferences conclude with teachers arranging for the continued development of positive relationships with the students in question.

## Extent of Use

TA is used by thousands of individuals in the helping professions, including psychologists and social workers. With the publication in 1972 of *Games Students Play* by Ken Ernst, teachers had an opportunity to understand how TA can be applied in classrooms.[12] Since that time workshops and courses on TA have become available throughout the United States. It is fair to say, however, that the approach is still identified primarily with individual therapy rather than classroom management.

## Assumptions

The basic assumption underlying TA is that every individual possesses three ego states, which Berne labels child, parent, and adult. At a given point in time when a person behaves in a certain way, he is guided by one of these ego states. Each has positive and negative qualities. Thus, the child ego state may be characterized by either creative and playful behavior or defiance and petulance. The parent state may be either nurturing and protective or prejudiced and authoritarian. The adult ego state is the least emotional, according to Berne. When exhibiting adult characteristics, an individual behaves logically and reasonably. These characteristics become undesirable when carried to the extreme of emotionlessness and insensitivity.

Problems tend to occur when individuals interact on the basis of different ego states. Since young people typically have less well-developed adult ego states, the likelihood is great that teachers will encounter occasions on which their students are operating from a different set of premises. When these incompatible interactions begin to occur according to a pattern, TA analysts contend that a "game" exists. Ernst identifies three such student games in classrooms: troublemaker games, put-down games, and temper games. He also describes three teacher games: close-to-student, helpful, and "I know best."

---

12 Ken Ernst, *Games Students Play* (Millbrae, Calif.: Celestial Arts, 1975). Information on TA workshops can be obtained by writing to the International Transactional Analysts Association, 1772 Vallejo St., P.O. Box 3932, Rincon Annex, San Francisco, CA 94119.

When TA is applied to classroom management, the assumption is that behavior problems can be reduced by making individuals aware of the origins of their behavior. The teacher is seen as the primary awareness agent. TA also assumes that once students understand their undesirable behavior, they will act to correct it.

## Potential Problems

Once again, the time required for individual contact with students may discourage some teachers from adopting TA. Relating to students in a "clinical" way often requires follow-up, particularly when students are in need of support or uncertain about how a teacher feels about them. Teachers also may feel uncomfortable in the role of clinician, particularly if at other times they must perform potentially conflicting roles, such as evaluator and disciplinarian.

---

### Key Questions

*TA places the teacher in the role of a clinician, observing undesirable student behavior and speculating on its origins. The questions a teacher would tend to ask are more analytical than instructional or organizational in nature.*

1. *What is the behavior I find troublesome?*
2. *Has this behavior occurred before?*
3. *What is the ego state of the student when he behaves this way and what is my ego state when I respond?*
4. *What is the gamelike nature of our interaction?*
5. *How can I communicate my perceptions to the student?*

---

## Summary

Nine approaches to classroom management and the resolution of behavior problems have been briefly introduced in Part I. They can be characterized by certain similarities and key differences. Before moving on to Part II, where these approaches are applied to actual classroom problems, it may be useful to review their goals, characteristics, and underlying assumptions.

Table 1 summarizes the basic goals. While advocates of each approach may argue that they seek other goals besides those listed, the check marks indicate the goals that appear to receive special emphasis. Perhaps it seems surprising that only three approaches concentrate on totally eliminating negative student

## TABLE 1 • GOALS

| | Assertive Discipline | Behavior Modification | Logical Consequences | Positive Peer Culture | Reality Therapy | Social Literacy | SMPSD | TET | TA |
|---|---|---|---|---|---|---|---|---|---|
| **Stop negative student behavior quickly** | ✓ | ✓ | | | | | | | ✓ |
| **Encourage responsible behavior** | | | ✓ | ✓ | ✓ | | ✓ | | |
| **Expand conflict-resolution capacity** | | | | | | ✓ | | ✓ | |
| **Improve teacher-student relations** | | | | | | ✓ | ✓ | ✓ | ✓ |
| **Increase feelings of teacher control** | ✓ | | | | | | | | |
| **Minimize problematic situations** | | | | | | | ✓ | | |
| **Restructure schools and/or classrooms** | | | ✓ | ✓ | ✓ | ✓ | ✓ | ✓ | |

## TABLE 2 • CHARACTERISTICS

| | Assertive Discipline | Behavior Modification | Logical Consequences | Positive Peer Culture | Reality Therapy | Social Literacy | SMPSD | TET | TA |
|---|---|---|---|---|---|---|---|---|---|
| Clear, well-communicated rules | ✓ | | | | | ✓ | ✓ | | |
| Punishments for inappropriate behavior | ✓ | ✓ | | | | | | | |
| Logical consequences | | | ✓ | | | | ✓ | | |
| Reinforcement of appropriate behavior | ✓ | ✓ | ✓ | | | | ✓ | | |
| Redefinition of teacher role | | | | ✓ | ✓ | | | ✓ | ✓ |

| | Assertive Discipline | Behavior Modification | Logical Consequences | Positive Peer Culture | Reality Therapy | Social Literacy | SMPSD | TET | TA |
|---|---|---|---|---|---|---|---|---|---|
| Group problem solving | | | ✓ | ✓ | ✓ | ✓ | ✓ | | |
| Negotiated conflict resolution | | | | | | ✓ | ✓ | ✓ | ✓ |
| Collaborative decision making for classroom rules | | | | ✓ | | ✓ | ✓ | ✓ | |
| Efforts to make students aware of origins of their behavior | | | ✓ | ✓ | ✓ | ✓ | | | ✓ |
| Parental involvement | | | | | | | ✓ | | |
| Team trouble-shooting | | | | | | | ✓ | | |

# TABLE 3 • ASSUMPTIONS

| Student Behavior is shaped by: | Assertive Discipline | Behavior Modification | Logical Consequences | Positive Peer Culture | Reality Therapy | Social Literacy | SMPSD | TET | TA |
|---|---|---|---|---|---|---|---|---|---|
| Teacher expectations | ✓ | | | | ✓ | | | | |
| Relationship with teacher | | | | | | | | | ✓ |
| Teacher communications | ✓ | | | | ✓ | ✓ | ✓ | ✓ | ✓ |
| School/classroom organization | | | | ✓ | | | ✓ | | |
| External reinforcement | | ✓ | | | | | | | |
| Existence of clear limits | ✓ | | ✓ | | | ✓ | ✓ | | |
| Academic achievement (or failure) | | | | | ✓ | | ✓ | | |

| | Assertive Discipline | Behavior Modification | Logical Consequences | Positive Peer Culture | Reality Therapy | Social Literacy | SMPSD | TET | TA |
|---|---|---|---|---|---|---|---|---|---|
| Teacher behavior is shaped by teacher attitudes | ✓ | | | | | | | | |
| Discipline need not entail "winners" and "losers" | | | | | | ✓ | | ✓ | |
| Behavior problems are normal and cannot be totally eliminated | | | | ✓ | | ✓ | ✓ | ✓ | |
| Rewards are not necessary for good behavior | | | | ✓ | | | | ✓ | |
| Student behavior is goal-directed | | ✓ | ✓ | | ✓ | | | | ✓ |
| Peer group can be a positive force | | | | ✓ | | ✓ | ✓ | | |

behavior, but many approaches view certain behavior problems as opportunities. Others assume that it is simply unrealistic to think of having no student behavior problems. Four approaches stress the acquisition of responsibility. The remaining goals center on the nature of interpersonal relations and school organization. The most radical approaches are those that call for restructuring schools and classrooms. Assertive Discipline, Behavior Modification, and Transactional Analysis are the least radical approaches, in that they do not require major changes in the structure of conventional schools and classrooms.

The prominent characteristics of the nine approaches are summarized in Table 2. Certain approaches emphasize relatively conventional aspects of classroom management — rules, punishments, and rewards. Others stress the importance of effective communications between teachers and students and student involvement in problem solving. Four approaches call on teachers to modify their role by undertaking more advising, counseling, and group facilitation. Parental involvement and teacher cooperation in diagnosing and resolving behavior problems characterize only one approach, the SMPSD. Many of the characteristics of the nine approaches require teachers to obtain special training.

Table 3 reviews some of the major assumptions that underlie the approaches. Since the methods entailed in each approach rest on these assumptions, it is critical for teachers to understand them before selecting an approach. Many of the assumptions concern factors influencing student behavior. Only Assertive Discipline emphasizes factors influencing teacher behavior. In reality, though, students and teachers exert simultaneous influences on each other's behavior. Four approaches assume that behavior problems and teacher-student conflicts can never be completely eliminated. The remaining approaches suggest that the right combination of teacher skills and resources can lead to the elimination of problems or the redefinition of problems as opportunities.

Having introduced the approaches and summarized their goals, characteristics, underlying assumptions, and potential problems, we shall now see how they can be applied to specific behavior problems that teachers encounter daily in classrooms. Each of the next six chapters will highlight a particular problem and several approaches. Chapter 9 then discusses how teachers may go about deciding which approach is best for them.

# P·A·R·T·T·W·O

# CLASSROOM APPLICATIONS

Understanding the goals, underlying assumptions, and characteristics of various approaches to classroom management is of little benefit unless teachers can envision how they actually might apply them to the resolution of behavior problems. With this objective in mind, we have selected six common behavior problems: poor attendance, incomplete assignments, use of controlled substances, aggressive behavior, student disrespect toward peers, and student disrespect toward teachers. Each of the next six chapters focuses on how to handle one of these concerns.

The format for each chapter is the same. After a brief introduction outlining the nature of the problematic behavior in question and an illustrative quotation in which a teacher talks about the problem, we focus on several of the nine approaches to classroom management and suggest how teachers employing them may handle the problem. An effort is made in each chapter to select two approaches that are widely divergent in how they would deal with the problem. To help you recall salient aspects of the approaches, a brief summary of each appears before it is discussed. The discussion utilizes the "Key Questions" introduced in Chapter 2 to suggest what a teacher employing one of the approaches would ask himself as he goes about resolving a class problem. By responding to each of these questions as a teacher might, we hope to portray what it actually would be like to implement each of the nine approaches to classroom management.

After a pair of approaches to each behavior problem has been highlighted, we compare them, pointing out possible strengths and weaknesses. Next comes a brief discussion of how other, nonhighlighted approaches might deal with the problem under consideration. Each chapter concludes with several review questions designed to help you reflect on the nature of the problem and the practical value of particular approaches for your own situation.

# ATTENDANCE
# PROBLEMS

Student failure to attend class can be extremely frustrating to elementary and secondary teachers for several reasons. First, when a student "skips" or "cuts" class without a legitimate excuse, he is often making a statement about his low regard for the subject matter, the teacher, classmates, his own performance in class, or some combination of the preceding. Second, the fact that attendance problems involve student *absence* means that it is more difficult to resolve the problem quickly. The student must be located, his excuse for being absent verified, and, in many cases, his parents notified. All of this takes time, and time is a very scarce commodity in most schools. A third reason why attendance problems frustrate teachers is that they frequently affect academic performance. Absent students miss classwork and assignments. Because absent students often are behind in their work to begin with, they easily can fall further behind and lose the motivation even to try to catch up. Teachers who want to help these students must invest considerable effort repeating instructions, explaining material, and checking work while the rest of the class moves ahead.

Attendance problems are a major source of concern throughout American public schools. Some inner-city schools have daily absence rates of 50 percent. In a survey of school administrators in New York and California, respondents reported that truancy, class cutting, and tardiness were their most serious discipline problems.[1] Since state funds for local schools typically are linked to

---

[1] Daniel L. Duke, "How Administrators View the Crisis in School Discipline," *Phi Delta Kappan*, Vol. 59, no. 5 (January 1978): 325–330.

daily attendance figures, student absenteeism can cost schools hundreds of thousands of dollars. The losses in terms of academic performance, however, are incalculable.

Teachers experience considerable uncertainty about how to handle attendance problems. Some teachers, particularly those with large classes, frankly admit that they are relieved when students are absent, especially when the students are ones who tend to be disruptive or demand a lot of time.[2] Others feel compelled to follow up on each absence but express guilt at devoting energy to students who are not in class when there are plenty of regular attenders deserving attention. Administrators are ambivalent about how to handle attendance problems. Some expect teachers to deal with class cutting, while others require attendance problems to be referred to the office. Many schools are characterized by great inconsistency in the reporting and handling of attendance problems. In this chapter we shall discuss several ways to deal with attendance problems.

## HANDLING CLASS CUTTING

The two approaches that will be applied to class cutting are Reality Therapy (pp. 23-26) and the Systematic Management Plan for School Discipline (pp. 29-32). One stresses student self-awareness of the problem, while the other seeks ways to alter organizational factors in order to reduce the likelihood that class cutting will occur. An individual teacher might employ Reality Therapy to help students understand why they decide not to attend class. The SMPSD, on the other hand, requires the involvement of various members of the school community. A basic issue, then, is whether or not class cutting can be dealt with in isolation.

The class-cutting problem with which we shall deal is expressed by our hypothetical teacher as follows:

> I don't know what to do with Dawn. She's so far behind in her work, yet she continues to miss class—at least one or two a week. I know she comes to school. And she never cuts art or music. If she continues to miss my class, she won't pass the course and she needs social studies.

While the problem as described takes place in a departmentalized secondary school, the discussion, in part, is equally appropriate for elementary schools. Instead of class cutting, the problem

---

[2] Daniel L. Duke and Adrienne M. Meckel, "The Slow Death of a Public High School," *Phi Delta Kappan*, Vol. 61, no. 10 (June 1980): 674-677.

in elementary school is more likely to be absenteeism from school, however. Of the two approaches, Reality Therapy probably has been used more with elementary-age students. Each approach is briefly summarized below.

## Reality Therapy

| | |
|---|---|
| Key: | Self-awareness |
| Central Assumption: | Student behavior problems often derive from low self-esteem |
| Goal: | Increase opportunities for students to feel good about themselves |
| Important Aspects: | Create groups in which students can discuss concerns and develop communication and awareness skills |
| | Eliminate activities that ensure some students will "fail" |
| | See that students make a formal commitment to overcome problems |
| Potential Problems: | Students may need to learn to deal with failure in a positive way for later life |
| | Reality Therapy can be time-consuming |
| | Teachers must be careful not to manipulate group meetings or make them "unsafe" |

## Systematic Management Plan for School Discipline

| | |
|---|---|
| Key: | Organizational change |
| Central Assumptions: | Problems are endemic to schools |

|  | Organizational factors determine behavior |
|---|---|
|  | Comprehensive—not piecemeal—change |
| Goals: | Address student behavior on a schoolwide basis |
|  | Establish organizational mechanisms for reducing problems |
| Important Aspects: | Understanding the school as a rule-governed organization |
|  | Data collection |
|  | Conflict resolution |
|  | Team troubleshooting |
|  | Parental involvement |
|  | Reinforcing environments for learning |
|  | Professional development |
| Potential Problems: | Requires careful coordination |
|  | SMPSD can be time-consuming |
|  | Commitment of resources may be necessary |

# Reality Therapy

## Key Questions

1. *Does this problem behavior relate to the student's academic history?*
2. *Does the student possess the skills and/or resources necessary to perform adequately in class?*
3. *Does the student understand the nature of the problem?*
4. *Is the student willing to make a commitment to correct the problem?*

*Does Dawn's class cutting relate to her academic history?* The teacher knows that Dawn is behind in her work, so there is some reason to suspect that academic problems play a role in her class cutting. When certain students fall too far behind, they tend to give up. Coming to class becomes too painful, a reminder that they are not meeting the teacher's expectations. Yet, without talking directly with Dawn, the teacher cannot be sure about her conjecture.

One alternative explanation for Dawn's class cutting is that she periodically has something else she prefers to do rather than attend social studies. For example, her boyfriend may have a free period. A second alternative is that Dawn may be upset with someone in her social studies class and is trying to avoid the person. This person could be a student or the teacher.

The teacher knows that Dawn is regularly attending art and music classes. The fact that she is not truant from all her classes suggests that the problem may be academic. Also, her selective attendance seems to preclude the possibility that her behavior is caused by serious problems outside school, since such problems probably would result in total nonattendance.

Before talking directly with Dawn to confirm her impressions, the teacher asks herself one additional question.

*Does Dawn possess the skills and/or resources necessary to perform adequately in class?* In checking the class roll book, the teacher notes that Dawn has been missing several classes a week since the beginning of the second semester. During second semester the work in social studies remained essentially the same as first semester — readings in the textbook, class lectures, and written homework based on end-of-chapter questions. The skills required to complete the coursework include a tenth-grade reading ability and the capacity to listen to lectures, take notes, and respond in writing to specific questions.

Dawn received a "C" grade at the end of the first semester, but it is clear that she possesses all the basic skills necessary to perform at a higher level in class. A review of her other first-semester grades reveals no grades lower than "C". Now, being reasonably certain that Dawn can complete her work in social studies if she wants to, the teacher talks directly to her.

*Does Dawn understand the nature of the problem?* At a private meeting with Dawn her teacher presents the problem for open, honest discussion. This kind of meeting should focus only on understanding and resolving the problem, not on punishment.

Dawn acknowledges that she has been cutting class and not completing her coursework. She is not very communicative, however.

Her teacher notes that she completed her assignments during the first semester and inquires about what has changed during second semester. After some assurances that she can be honest without fear of reprisals or angry reactions, Dawn begins to open up. She expresses hurt over her first-semester grade. She feels she worked very hard, completed her assignments on time, and took careful notes. She expected a "B". When she received a "C" she could not understand why she had been given the mark. She figured no matter how hard she tried, she could do no better than an average grade. For Dawn, the problem derives from the teacher, not from missing class. She feels rejected and the victim of unfair grading.

It is not always possible to achieve full understanding of a problem in one such meeting; several may be required. Scheduling meetings is not always easy. When time is unavailable during class, meetings may have to be arranged for planning periods, before school, during study hall, or after school. At the point where both teacher and student arrive at a common understanding of the problem, it is appropriate to elicit a formal commitment from the student to correct the problem.

*Is Dawn willing to make a commitment to correct the problem?* Dawn's trust in her social studies teacher — and her own competence — has been shaken by the unexpected low grade at the end of first semester. It is also possible that the teacher's feelings have been hurt by the discovery that Dawn thinks she has graded her unfairly. It will take time to rebuild trust between the two. Initially, Dawn is reluctant to make a commitment to attend class regularly. Dawn is asked, "If you won't sign a paper saying you will try to attend class regularly, will you sign a paper saying you will not sign a paper?" Again, she is reluctant to agree.

The purpose of this process is to start Dawn thinking about what it means to make a commitment. She is asked, "Will you permit your name to be placed on a list indicating that you will neither agree nor refuse to come to class regularly?" Dawn grudgingly gives her consent. Dawn is being afforded an opportunity to express her upset without encountering teacher anger or reprisals. In time Dawn's trust will grow and she may be less reluctant to make a written commitment to attend class regularly. Such a formal statement may not even be necessary, however, since she probably will begin to attend class on her own. Glasser reminds teachers that, for all their apparent disinterest in school, most students actually desire to feel needed by their teachers and welcome in class.

### Glasser with Groups

We presented an example of how Reality Therapy might work with one student. In one of his books, Glasser also discusses how groups can be handled. He reports working with one eighth-grade class in which six to eight students routinely missed school. Meeting with the entire class of thirty-five students, he initiated the first step of his approach—exposing the problem for open, honest discussion. After the problem had been discussed, Glasser worked on getting commitment—commitment from regular attenders to help remind nonattenders and commitment from nonattenders to come to school. As in the case of Dawn, commitment was slow in coming, but the process of group problem solving had been started. Students were exposed to the idea of personal responsibility and commitment. They were made aware that the teacher was unwilling to step in and try to solve the class-cutting problem unilaterally. Students were placed in a situation where they were expected to assume some responsibility for helping each other.

## Systematic Management Plan for School Discipline (SMPSD)

### Key Questions

1. *Does this behavior problem occur frequently?*
2. *If the problem is chronic, under what circumstances does it occur?*
3. *Are there any characteristics of classroom or school organization (such as how rules or consequences are decided, how conflicts are resolved, etc.) that might contribute to the problem?*
4. *In what ways can the problem be addressed on a comprehensive, schoolwide basis (involving teachers, students, parents, etc.)?*

*Does this problem occur frequently?* In order to discuss class cutting and how the SMPSD deals with it, we must modify the problem statement a bit. The SMPSD is an approach geared to chronic
problems involving more than one student. Let us assume that
Dawn is not alone. Class cutting therefore is a problem about
which a number of teachers complain.

*If class cutting is chronic, under what circumstances does it occur?*
In order to answer the question a meeting of the entire faculty and
administration is necessary. Such a meeting can be called by a concerned teacher, but she should work through official channels,
since administrative support is essential to the development of a
workable plan for handling class cutting. When the meeting is
held, teachers report that cutting occurs at various times but that
the problem seems to be greatest during first and fifth periods.
Some teachers also report greater class cutting on the day of a test.

Further probing reveals that certain teachers have more cuts than
others. These teachers tend to have "core" academic courses rather
than electives and require frequent homework and classwork.

Following the meeting with teachers and administrators a
group of students is asked to share their observations of class cutting. They agree that cuts seem to be greatest during first and fifth
periods and cite a variety of explanations. They also mention that
several teachers never report students who miss class without per-
mission. These tend to be teachers of lower-ability students.

*Are there any characteristics of classroom or school organization
that might contribute to class cutting?* The results of our fact-
finding efforts suggest that there probably is no single cause of
class cutting.

First-period cuts may be explained in part as a function of the
roll-taking policy of the school. Students who do not appear in
first-period class are listed as absent. Once recorded as absent,
they are free to attend whichever classes they want. It is specu-
lated that the parental excuses they bring to school on the day following their reported absence are often forged.

Fifth-period cuts likely have a different origin. Fifth period follows lunch. Students are free to eat lunch off campus if they desire.
Possibly some students who leave campus are enjoying themselves
so much that they choose to extend their lunch another period.

The fact that teachers of "core" academic courses seem to have
more cuts does not necessarily mean that organizational factors

are to blame. It is possible, for example, that individuals who teach electives tend to have a different attitude toward attendance than those who teach required courses. We still lack sufficient information on the students who cut these classes to speculate about reasons.

If many of the students who cut class turn out to be having difficulty understanding their assignments, teachers may need to clarify directions and provide more direct supervision of student work. Lower-ability students are particularly susceptible to frustration when the reasons for classwork are vague or they lack regular teacher monitoring. This frustration can serve as an impetus to class cutting.

As for the students' report that some teachers fail to turn in the names of those who cut class, it appears that there is no way at present that the administration can identify these teachers. No policies exist governing the collection of data on class attendance other than first-period roll. Teachers are told to report all suspected cuts, but there is little way for administrators to monitor the process under the current system.

*In what ways can class cutting be addressed on a comprehensive, schoolwide basis?* The multiplicity of organizational factors possibly contributing to class cutting justifies comprehensive, schoolwide corrective action. The first need is for more systematic monitoring of class cutting. Instead of being collected only during first period, class attendance forms should be collected every period. A list of students reported absent during first period can be put together and distributed to teachers each day. Teachers can then identify any students who are present but who cut first period. In addition, office personnel can compare the rolls from each succeeding period with first-period roll to determine which students are cutting class. Students found to be missing from class can be reported immediately to their parents. This latter policy may reduce fifth-period cuts substantially.

Collecting and processing class attendance data for every period and notifying parents require considerable time and energy. Either existing staff must reallocate their time or additional personnel have to be obtained. It is possible that parent volunteers can be used effectively to assist in monitoring class cutting.

Systematic data collection may lead to the identification of teachers who routinely fail to report students for cutting class. Once identified, these teachers may need to be counseled on the potential dangers of allowing students to cut. One such danger is that students will interpret the action as an "I don't care about you" message from the teacher. Another danger is that nonenforcement will lead other students to cut class. Students who miss class increase the likelihood that they will fall behind in their work.

If some students are cutting class because the classwork is too difficult, teachers may need to pool their energies and provide remediation. Team teaching is one organizational strategy that allows two or more teachers to combine their classes for purposes of dividing labor. While one teacher concentrates on working individually with a few students who are having difficulty keeping up, another teacher can conduct large-group instruction.

A final organizational change we may wish to consider involves the consequences for students who cut class. Chronic class cutting often is punished by suspension from school. Such a sanction in reality may function as a reward! If a student is missing class already, compelling him to miss more classes is not necessarily a wise course of action. Instead, a policy calling for the student to make up missed time on Saturday or after school may be more sensible. It also may be useful to involve students in the determination of such a policy, since they are likely to have a better sense of what consequences for cutting class will be most effective.

## Comparing Approaches

As previously indicated, the two approaches highlighted in this chapter focus on different levels of action. Glasser's methods are aimed at individuals and small groups. The SMPSD is designed for schoolwide action where problems are fairly widespread. Both approaches, however, assume that problems like class cutting will never be totally eliminated. Therefore, they stress techniques for increasing an understanding of the circumstances surrounding class cutting.

The strength of the Reality Therapy approach lies in its immediate utility. When a problem such as class cutting occurs, a teacher can employ the techniques to establish communications with a student or group of students. By drawing out student feelings and enlisting students in the search for solutions, the approach not only may help alleviate the problem, but it also attempts to encourage the growth of responsible behavior. The teacher employing Reality Therapy ideas does not exercise a monopoly over the resolution of behavior problems.

The SMPSD also provides opportunities for students to develop responsibility. Students are involved in determining rules, the consequences for disobeying them, and ways to prevent problems from recurring. Unlike Glasser's approach, however, the SMPSD takes time to be implemented. Stress is placed on developing the capability of groups of people to manage and reduce behavior problems in general, rather than to respond to particular problems when they arise. The SMPSD calls for team diagnosis and planning, systematic data collection, and ongoing troubleshooting.

The potential value of a comprehensive approach like the SMPSD was demonstrated in a study of illegal absenteeism in two urban secondary schools.[3] Despite the existence of rules prohibiting truancy, tardiness, and class cutting and punishments in the event students disobeyed the rules, rates of illegal absenteeism remained high at both schools. A year's investigation revealed a variety of organizational problems that reduced the capacity of school personnel to deal effectively with absenteeism. Some examples may be instructive:

1. New attendance policies were introduced without first checking to see if they were feasible. Efforts were not made to solicit faculty input or approval.
2. No provision was made for the continuous supervision of the campus.
3. The reporting of student absences was unsystematic.
4. Little attempt was made to verify whether students were legally absent or not.
5. Rules were not consistently enforced and consequences for disobeying them were not consistently administered.

In deciding on an appropriate classroom management approach, the above research suggests that teachers should look beyond the four walls of their own room. Concerning yourself exclusively with how to handle your own problems ultimately may undercut efforts to generate effective schoolwide policies. It may take more time and energy to obtain the commitment of the entire faculty, but in the long run the investment could be worth it.

Thus far we have highlighted two somewhat distinct approaches. How do they compare to the other seven where attendance problems are concerned?

3 Daniel L. Duke and Adrienne M. Meckel, "Student Attendance Problems and School Organization: A Case Study," *Urban Education*, Vol. 15, no. 3 (October 1980): 325–357.

Glasser's approach probably is more similar to TET than any other. Both entail talking with individual students to determine how to handle problems. Logical Consequences and TA make an effort to increase student understanding of a problem's origins, but both stop short of prescribing specific ways to go about resolving the problem. While the techniques for eliciting student understanding are similar to those used in the preceding approaches, Positive Peer Culture and Social Literacy Training are oriented primarily toward groups, rather than individuals. Peer influence is used to increase understanding of problems and guide behavior change. Positive Peer Culture, in fact, might call on students to see to it that their class-cutting friends begin to attend class on a regular basis.

Assertive Discipline and Behavior Modification tend to focus more on rules and sanctions than interpersonal dialogue and awareness building. Students who cut the class of a teacher using Assertive Discipline are subject to punishment. There is little opportunity for teacher-student consultation. Behavior Modification may call for a system for reinforcing students when they attend class and punishing or withdrawing privileges when they fail to attend. Dreikurs' approach also is concerned with the consequences of student misconduct. Using suspension from school or class to "punish" a student who cuts class would be criticized by Dreikurs as an illogical consequence, however. A more logical consequence may be to deny the student a chance to make up any work he missed when he was illegally absent.

Assertive Discipline and Behavior Modification really are quite different from the other approaches in that they assume students will correct their behavior without having an opportunity to discuss it. One possible shortcoming of these two approaches is the fact that absenteeism may be a symptom of student dissatisfaction with school. Imposing punishments for class cutting without trying to understand the reasons behind it may only serve to make school *more* dissatisfying. If, on the other hand, students cut class because they wish to do something more enjoyable, the use of some form of punishment may be effective in curtailing the behavior.

The examples discussed in this chapter relate primarily to secondary schools. Illegal absenteeism tends to be far less of a problem at the elementary level. When it occurs, it may be due more to school phobia or fear of the teacher than to factors associated with secondary school absenteeism. These factors include lack of interest in school or in particular classes, frustration related to poor performance, and the presence of more desirable alternatives.

Given the somewhat different etiology of school absenteeism for younger students, elementary teachers may find approaches that stress student understanding and discussion more appropriate than those emphasizing rewards and sanctions. Important at any age, parental involvement in the case of elementary school absenteeism becomes crucial. The fact that most elementary teachers work all day in self-contained classrooms with the same students makes it easier to coordinate parental contacts and provide time for individual student conferences and group problem solving. Teachers in secondary schools with days divided into forty- to fifty-minute periods generally have less flexibility.

## Activities

1. Think about the various reasons why a student might cut class. List them. Is it important to know why a student has cut class in order to decide how to deal with him?
2. This chapter deals with class cutting. Another attendance problem is tardiness (coming to class late). Speculate on how each of the nine approaches might handle tardiness.
3. Every teacher has his or her own style of dealing with problems. Is Reality Therapy an approach you would feel comfortable using with a student like Dawn? Discuss ways in which Reality Therapy conforms to and deviates from your personal style of classroom management.
4. Describe the possibilities and/or limitations of implementing the SMPSD in your school. What aspects of school organization might need to be changed in order to reduce illegal absenteeism?
5. Lists of questions a teacher might ask accompany both approaches highlighted in this chapter. If you were confronted by a student who was illegally absent from your class, what questions would you ask yourself? Do these questions resemble those of any of the nine approaches (refer to Chapter 2)?

# INCOMPLETE ASSIGNMENTS

While failure to complete an assignment is rarely mentioned in the same breath as truancy or fighting, it nevertheless represents a classroom management problem with which both elementary and secondary teachers periodically must deal. Outside assistance, frequently available for other behavior problems, is generally unavailable for cases involving incomplete assignments. Teachers are on their own.

Incomplete assignments range from work that students never begin to work that is undertaken but only partially completed. The causes of incomplete assignments vary widely and may need to be investigated by the teacher desiring to reduce the frequency of incomplete assignments. Some students fail to complete assignments because they lack the requisite skills or knowledge. Other students do not organize their time wisely, budgeting too much time for some work and too little for other work. Still others find themselves in situations where for one reason or another it is difficult to get work done. Reasons include disturbances from other people, lack of proper materials, inadequate study space, and unanticipated emergencies.

Failure to complete assignments for the reasons listed above may require different teacher responses from those called for when students do not even try to get their work done. Failing to try at all—like class cutting—may indicate that students have other activities besides schoolwork that they prefer to do or that they resent being required to do any work.

It is impossible to estimate the extent to which failure to complete assignments causes problems for teachers. Accurate statistics on such matters simply are not systematically maintained. We suspect, though, that the problem is pervasive and that teachers can be adversely affected in several ways simultaneously. First, when a student does not complete an assignment, his action may be interpreted by the teacher as a manifestation of apathy or disregard. Such "messages" contribute to teacher job dissatisfaction. Second, incomplete work adds to the teacher's workload. Even if the teacher refuses to allow the student to make up his "incomplete," she still must deal with the fact that he has not covered certain material. If the material is crucial to advancement, the teacher may be compelled to see that the student covers it in some other way. In classes where incomplete assignments are common, teachers encounter massive bookkeeping chores as they try to keep track of which students are missing which assignments.

# HANDLING INCOMPLETE ASSIGNMENTS

In this chapter, we discuss in detail how two approaches — Teacher Effectiveness Training (pp. 33–36) and Behavior Modification (pp. 14–17) — might deal with failure to complete assignments. The problem is expressed in such a way that it could characterize either an elementary or a secondary classroom. Following the description of TET and Behavior Modification, we briefly review how other approaches might treat failure to complete assignments.

The problem of incomplete assignments is expressed by our hypothetical teacher as follows:

> Martin is funny about his work. Sometimes he'll go for two weeks and finish everything. Then, he won't work in class or finish any homework. I tell him that he can't pass math unless he does his classwork and homework. He'll work for a while and I'll praise him for getting his work done. Then the problem comes up again. He seems to understand math all right. And he doesn't disturb others when he is not working. He just makes up his mind he isn't going to do any work. I don't know what's really bothering him. It's too bad. He could excel if he put his mind to it.

TET and Behavior Modification are an interesting pair of approaches to compare, since the former places no emphasis on the use of reinforcement, while the latter is based on the belief that virtually all behavior is governed by rewards and sanctions. TET stresses the quality of communications between teachers and students. Both approaches share one common characteristic, however. Rather than dwelling on the "root causes" of a problem, they zero in on how to resolve the problem. Each approach is briefly summarized below:

## Teacher Effectiveness Training

| | |
|---|---|
| Key: | Teacher communications |
| Central Assumptions: | No one can be *forced* to do anything |
| | Problems cannot be totally eliminated |
| Goals: | "No-lose" conflict resolution |
| | Less provocative teacher talk |
| Important Aspects: | "I-messages" |
| | "Owning" the problem |
| | Six-step problem-resolution process |
| | Active listening |
| Potential Problems: | Problem resolution can be time-consuming |
| | Teachers may have to change their values on occasion |
| | Students may "test" the negotiations process |

## Behavior Modification

| | |
|---|---|
| Key: | Reinforcement |
| Central Assumptions: | Students misbehave because the consequences of misbehavior are reinforcing |
| Goals: | Decrease negative behavior |
| | Increase positive behavior |

Important Aspects: Rewarding desirable behavior is more effective than punishing undesirable behavior

Ignore attention-seeking misconduct

Avoid expecting dramatic changes in behavior

Potential Problems: Not all misbehavior may be attention seeking

Behavior modification overlooks an understanding of the root causes of behavior problems

Finding adequate reinforcers for other students may be difficult

# Teacher Effectiveness Training (TET)

### Key Questions
1. *What is the problem and who "owns" it?*
2. *Is there agreement by Martin that a problem exists?*
3. *What is the nature of communications between Martin and the teacher?*
4. *How can the problem be resolved in such a way as to strengthen the relationship between Martin and the teacher?*

*What is the problem and who "owns" it?* As expressed in the opening description, the problem is the teacher's. Martin is not completing enough work to enable her — given her standards — to give him a passing grade. The teacher is frustrated because she suspects that Martin has the mental ability to do what is expected of him. She does not understand why Martin goes for several weeks without missing an assignment and then ceases to work. TET does not require, however, that the teacher be aware of the underlying causes of a problem. It is sufficient if the immediate problem can be described accurately. In TET emphasis is placed primarily on resolving the problem to the satisfaction of all parties involved.

Stating that Martin's penchant for incomplete work is his teacher's problem does not preclude the possibility that there are problems in Martin's life as well. It merely indicates that Martin does not feel sufficiently uncomfortable about the missed assignments to raise them as an issue. It is likely he would be content to continue his pattern of behavior indefinitely. His teacher, though, has reached a point where she feels she must do more than warn Martin of the consequences of his behavior. Apparently, her strategy of periodic admonitions has not been effective.

*Is there agreement by Martin that a problem exists?* According to Thomas Gordon, it is crucial that the teacher determine whether or not Martin understands why she views his periodic failure to complete work as a problem. Without this understanding, there can be no basis for negotiating a "no-lose" solution to the problem.

The teacher should be careful initially to use an "I-message" to express the problem to Martin. If she describes the problem as Martin's rather than her own, she may subvert her efforts by placing Martin on the defensive. The following statements are illustrative of an "I-message" and a "you-message":

> *Preferred statement*
>
> I have a problem you can help me with. I am worried that you will not pass algebra if you continue to leave work undone. It upsets me to see my students fail when they have the ability to pass. I feel as if I have failed when this happens. Teaching loses its pleasure for me.

> *Less desirable statement*
>
> You've failed to complete your assignments again, Martin. This has happened too many times this year. You're going to fail if you don't get your work done, and there'll be no one to blame but yourself.

Using an "I-message" increases the likelihood that Martin will come to regard his behavior as annoying if not for himself at least for his teacher. Let us assume that Martin listens to the "I-message" and agrees that his periodic failure to complete work is disturbing the teacher and that something needs to be done.

*What is the nature of communications between Martin and the teacher?* The teacher needs to ask herself this question in order to help facilitate the next step — the actual attempt to resolve the problem. Reflecting on her interactions with Martin over the year, she acknowledges that she has not talked very much with Martin about his behavior. Nor has she listened to his feelings about her, the class, or the assignments. Usually, she has felt pressed by other work and has simply told Martin that he will not pass mathematics if he does not do all the assignments. The teacher tends to be "all business" in class. She believes Martin is old enough to be responsible for getting his work done. Besides, she does not feel she has the time to stand over every student to make sure work is done or to call home every time an assignment is not turned in.

"Active listening," one of the cornerstones of effective interpersonal relations, has not characterized the teacher's behavior toward Martin. It is conceivable that the lack of opportunities for Martin to express his feelings to the teacher and be heard has contributed to his pattern of on-again/off-again work.

*How can the problem be resolved in such a way as to strengthen the relationship between Martin and the teacher?* The way the last key question is phrased is interesting. It suggests that the primary goal of resolving the present problem is improving the relationship between Martin and his teacher, not getting him to complete all of his assignments or pass mathematics. According to the philosophy of TET, everything that occurs in class derives in large part from the nature of the relationship between the teacher and individual students. The key to these relationships, in turn, is the quality of communications between teacher and students.

As a result of asking herself the preceding question, the teacher realizes how her interactions with Martin have been deficient in active listening and possibly ineffective in terms of their desired outcome. In order to implement the six-step problem-resolution process that constitutes the heart of TET, she must work on hearing what Martin has to say. The object of active listening in this instance is to achieve a solution that satisfies both Martin's needs and the teacher's needs.

The first step of the problem-resolution process, the determination of the problem and who owns it, already has been accomplished as a result of the opening query. The teacher has asked Martin to have lunch with her and discuss the matter in a constructive way. Now comes step two, the generation of possible solutions to the problem. Martin and the teacher brainstorm possible solutions with each taking a turn describing one but exercising care not to make any judgments about particular solutions. During his turns, Martin suggests the following solutions.

1. Teacher reduces number of assignments.
2. Teacher bases class grade on a final exam, not on classwork and homework.
3. Teacher allows Martin to make up past assignments that were not completed.
4. Teacher schedules individual review sessions with Martin.
5. Teacher sends Martin to the office when he doesn't complete his assignments.

During her turns, the teacher recommends these alternative courses of action:

1. Martin works on math with another teacher.
2. Martin cannot move on to a new activity until he finishes the current assignment.
3. Martin stays in class but plans to take math again in summer school.
4. Martin is teamed up with a group of three classmates, all of whom share responsibility for seeing that they complete their work.
5. Teacher phones Martin's parents every time he fails to complete an assignment.

When Martin and his teacher have run out of alternative solutions, they are ready to move to step three, the evaluation of the solutions. Each goes through the list and eliminates any possible solutions that are completely unacceptable. It is hoped that at least one solution will remain which Martin and the teacher can agree to try. If all alternatives are rejected, the two must return to step two and try to develop other solutions.

Martin and the teacher decide (step four) that they will try one of his suggestions—scheduling regular review sessions so that Martin's teacher can check to see how his work is going. Step five entails determining how to implement the solution. As in the previous steps, this decision must be a joint enterprise. Martin and the teacher agree to meet every Friday during the last ten minutes of class. Martin will have his math classwork and homework available for these meetings, along with any questions about the assignments. For the final step, the two decide to evaluate how the solution is working in three weeks. If Martin still fails to complete a number of assignments, it will be necessary to reinstitute the problem-solving process and generate a new list of alternatives.

The last statement illustrates a critical dimension of TET. If a proposed solution fails to correct the problem behavior, the problem-solving process is tried again. It is inappropriate for the teacher to intervene after one or two failures and dictate a solution. To do so would be to undermine the credibility of the negotiations process, which is premised on the belief that students will not learn to behave responsibly as long as teachers feel they must singlehandedly resolve all difficult problems. Thus, as "inefficient" or time-consuming as it may be to repeat the problem-resolution process, teachers should be prepared to share authority with students.

## Behavior Modification

Key Questions
1. *What is the specific behavior that requires modification?*
2. *When does the behavior occur?*
3. *What are the immediate consequences of this behavior?*
4. *How can these consequences serve to reinforce the behavior?*
5. *How can the consequences be altered?*
6. *How can appropriate behavior be reinforced in the future?*

*What is the specific behavior that requires modification?* Martin periodically fails to do his mathematics classwork and homework.

*When does the behavior occur?* Every two weeks or so Martin stops completing his assignments.

*What are the immediate consequences of this behavior?* The teacher asks Martin if he understands the math concepts he is required to use. Martin indicates that he does. The teacher gets upset and threatens Martin with the prospect of failing mathematics.

*How can these consequences serve to reinforce the behavior?* Teacher attention, even when it is critical, can be reinforcing to some students. If Martin is feeling neglected — either in school or elsewhere — he may seek visible and audible evidence that someone he respects cares about him. Whenever he stops completing his assignments, he has discovered that his teacher registers concern and gets upset — two potent signs of caring.

*How can the consequences be altered?*

*How can appropriate behavior be reinforced in the future?* Martin's teacher can stop providing concerned attention when he fails to complete his work. Instead, she can withdraw a privilege or introduce a punishment (such as detention after school until the missing work is completed). In other words, she can remove the reinforcing consequences of Martin's behavior.

At the same time, the teacher can begin to provide attention when Martin does complete his work. Rather than taking such behavior for granted, she can treat finished classwork and homework as important occasions for praise, a phone call home, or, periodically, perhaps an inexpensive treat. If Martin's teacher emphasizes punishment or withdrawal of privileges to the exclusion of reinforcing appropriate behavior, she runs the risk that Martin will begin to avoid her or grow resentful and hostile.

## Comparing Approaches

It may seem striking to some teachers that the preceding applications of TET and Behavior Modification did not stress why Martin periodically failed to do his assignments or why he might need attention. Gordon assumes that Martin will share his feelings about the behavior during the problem-resolution process if he wants to. Whether or not he does, however, the problem must be resolved. Gordon believes that stressing problem resolution rather than problem diagnosis gives a more positive quality to the interactions between students and teachers.

Behavior Modification, along with Assertive Discipline, share a similar emphasis on resolution rather than diagnosis. Both approaches also stress the value of reinforcing appropriate behavior. Assertive Discipline, like TET, seeks to meet both the teacher's needs and the student's needs. Toward this end, however, Assertive Discipline is much more likely to utilize punishment than either Behavior Modification or TET. A teacher using Assertive Discipline with Martin probably would make sure he understood the rules regarding completion of work and the consequences for disobeying the rules. The first time thereafter that Martin failed to complete an assignment, he would receive a warning. Additional infractions would be punished, probably by detention, office referral and parental contact, or grade reduction.

With the exception of the SMPSD, the remaining five approaches to classroom management make some provision for helping Martin and his teacher become clear about why he periodically fails to complete his work. Positive Peer Culture and Social Literacy might call on the teacher to engage the entire class in the act of helping Martin. Logical Consequences, Reality Therapy, and Transactional Analysis tend to be less group-oriented.

With Logical Consequences, the teacher speculates on which of four primary motives (attention getting, power, revenge, or inadequacy) has influenced Martin. The assumption is not automatically made, as was the case with Behavior Modification, that Martin seeks attention. Martin is confronted with the teacher's diagnosis and given an opportunity to discuss his feelings. At the same time, he can be made aware that his behavior has certain natural consequences, namely that he will not be able to pass mathematics.

With Reality Therapy, Glasser would urge the teacher to help Martin become aware of the origins of his behavior. Unlike Logical Consequences, this approach does not specify general causal categories, though. Martin's behavior could be due to one or more factors, including the following:

1. Lack of appreciation for how math will be of benefit in later life.
2. Periodic inability to concentrate due to problems outside school.
3. Physical problems impairing concentration.
4. Periodic presence of activities that are sufficiently exciting to justify missing assignments.
5. Lack of clarity about directions for completing the assignment.
6. Resentment toward the teacher over lack of individual contact.

Once Martin becomes more aware of why he periodically fails to complete assignments, he will be in a better position to commit himself to a corrective course of action. TET differs from Reality Therapy primarily in the latter's insistence on student awareness.

TA is the most clinical of the approaches, implying that more time and effort would be devoted to making Martin aware of why he is failing to complete all of his work than to generating solutions to the problem. The teacher might ask Martin what he "gets" out of periodically failing to do his math work. Sometimes, for example, students receive satisfaction or recognition by creating problems. If both Martin and his teacher discover that such benefits accrue from his negative behavior, they can try to create alternative situations in which satisfaction and recognition result from positive behavior.

The SMPSD approach is primarily concerned with behavior problems that occur among many students or with the same student in different situations. If Martin's teacher were committed to the SMPSD and working in a departmentalized school, she might inquire among his other teachers to determine if he had failed to complete work in their classes as well. If so, it would be sensible to develop a coordinated strategy supported by all of Martin's teachers. She could also check with his parents to see if he completed work at home. If he fails to complete work only in math, the teacher might consider what aspects of her math teaching, interpersonal style, or subject matter might be contributing to Martin's behavior. In addition, one of the other classroom management approaches that assists students in discussing the origins of their behavior might be employed. Use of the SMPSD does not preclude employing other approaches as well.

## Activities

1. List ways in which aspects of a given body of subject matter can contribute to student failure to complete assignments (the curriculum might be too challenging, not challenging enough, or irrelevant). Propose strategies for modifying the curriculum in order to reduce the likelihood of incomplete assignments.
2. Another problem related to student work habits is plagiarism. Would you deal with plagiarism in a manner different from failure to complete assignments? Describe how the nine approaches might approach the issue of plagiarism.
3. A critical component of TET is the use of "I-messages." Find a colleague and role-play different situations in which

a teacher is faced with a student behavior problem. Practice communicating concern to the student using "I-messages."

4. Interview a group of your colleagues. Ask them to identify situations when they fail to complete their work. Ask them the reasons for this behavior. How do these reasons compare with the reasons discussed in this chapter?

5. List ten different rewards or privileges that you could use to reinforce students who complete their assignments. What problems would you encounter in using these rewards?

# SMOKING, DRINKING, DRUGS

Schools and their surrounding communities are inseparable. What affects one affects the other. School personnel often complain that they are asked to deal with problems that spill onto campus from the adjacent community. Problems that parents and community leaders are reluctant to deal with are thrust upon teachers and administrators.

One such case is the increasing use and abuse of cigarettes, alcohol, marijuana, and other drugs by young people. A recent HEW study, for example, reports that within the past five years, high school seniors have nearly doubled their daily intake of marijuana and are using a form of marijuana that has increased in potency.[1] The HEW report also notes that more than 30 percent of the seniors said they used marijuana before the ninth grade. Similar statistics are available for heavy alcohol consumption.[2] Students are using more and beginning at earlier ages. Suspensions of students caught smoking on California campuses have reached such proportions that administrators are establishing "designated smoking areas" to cut down on lost revenue.

The evidence on the effects of drug use on young bodies and minds is mixed and incomplete, but there are strong indications that many drugs have a deleterious effect on learning and motor

---

[1] *National Institute on Drug Abuse Report* (Washington, D.C.: Department of Health, Education and Welfare, 1980).

[2] Ruth C. Engs, *Responsible Drug and Alcohol Use* (New York: Macmillan Publishing Company, 1979), p. 48.

coordination.[3] It is too soon to predict the long-term consequences of using these substances for the current generation of heavier users, but negative social by-products are likely. On school campuses users and nonusers alike must use the same classrooms and facilities. Students who are "high," for instance, may respond poorly to class activities and become involved in behavior problems more easily. Student drug users may engage in verbal and physical harassment to convince nonusers to experiment with drugs. Such problems can cause some students to avoid attending school or to restrict their participation in school activities. Also, drug use can lead to theft and extortion and to the presence of undesirable strangers on campus.

Students and adults alike worry about the negative influence of peers, but peer pressure is not the only reason why students turn to drugs. Students are members of an ever-changing society and are susceptible to many of the stresses and strains adults encounter. Young people may start using drugs as a coping mechanism, only to discover that reliance on drugs creates new problems. On the other hand, some evidence indicates that the social drug user is as different from the drug abuser as the social drinker is from the alcoholic.[4] Knowing that a student is experimenting casually with drugs may or may not be cause for serious concern.

Often these problems seem so complex that it is difficult for teachers to know where to begin. In many cases teachers adopt strategies such as problem avoidance or problem acceptance.[5] Problem avoidance is a deliberate decision not to deal with problematic behavior, typically because of feelings of helplessness or a belief that intervention might lead to worse problems. Teachers in one study reported that they did not patrol areas known to be sites of illegal student activities.[6] The areas generally avoided included group meeting places where cigarettes and marijuana

3 *Ibid*, pp. 67–72 and 194–210. Engs notes that research reports often contradict one another regarding the potential harmful effects of drugs — especially in the case of marijuana. However, Engs does believe there is fairly conclusive evidence that marijuana may cause lung damage, does increase cardiac problems for those susceptible to heart ailments, and may impair driving ability (pp. 209–210).

4 Daniel Yankelovich, "How Students Control Their Drug Crisis," *Psychology Today*, October 1975, pp. 39–42.

5 Daniel L. Duke and Adrienne M. Meckel, *Managing Student Behavior Problems* (New York: Teachers College Press, 1980), pp. 6–11.

6 Daniel L. Duke, "Adults Can Be Discipline Problems Too!" *Psychology in the Schools*, Vol. 15, no. 4 (October 1978): 522–528.

were exchanged. Teachers apparently felt that they should not jeopardize their own safety by doing "police" work.

Problem acceptance, on the other hand, describes situations in which behavior that once was regarded as unacceptable is reconsidered and labeled acceptable. The repeal of Prohibition and the decriminalization of marijuana possession in Alaska are notable examples of problem acceptance. An individual teacher may feel that students ought to have access to campus smoking areas because she is allowed to smoke cigarettes on campus and "double standards" ought not to exist. The teacher who agrees with student values may tolerate smoking or other drug use and not enforce school rules banning such behavior.

Problem avoidance and acceptance, however, are difficult strategies to defend when students are involved in behaviors defined as criminal acts. Teachers may be legally liable in cases where they have condoned illegal student actions.

How and when to deal with student drug use is unclear. It is not always easy to determine whether a student has been smoking, drinking, or using drugs. False accusations can do considerable harm to students and place teachers in a legally vulnerable position. It is often the case that drug-related behaviors occur when groups of students gather. Under such conditions, it may be difficult to know which students actually are smoking or drinking and which are merely observing the activity. Should the students who supplied the drugs be given a stiffer penalty than the student consumers? How is the bystander to be treated?

The difficulty of knowing how and when to act is compounded by the problem of conflicting values related to drug use. Some educators are so fearful of drug abuse they have proposed compulsory urine testing and in-depth family questionnaires to identify drug users.[7] Others oppose such identification programs because they worry that students who are labeled drug users may have less opportunity to change their behavior.

## HANDLING A DRUG PROBLEM

Physical safety, legal liability, and value issues combine to make problems involving smoking, drinking, and drugs particularly resistant to efforts by individual teachers. Schoolwide approaches

---

[7] "Are Our Schools Creating Drug Abusers?" *American School Board Journal*, Vol. 161, no. 1 ( January 1974): 12–13.

may offer greater potential for success because they encourage participation from all role groups and provide opportunities for dialogue. In the case of issues such as drug use and abuse, school-wide discussion can dispel myths held by adults and students alike. Cooperative efforts also are more likely to generate the additional resources — in time, energy, and personnel — necessary for complex problem solving. For these reasons, Social Literacy Training (pp. 77–79) and the Systematic Management Plan for School Discipline (pp. 79–81) are highlighted in this chapter. Each approach is briefly summarized below.

The problem that will be addressed by Social Literacy Training and the SMPSD is described in the vignette at the end of this paragraph. It involves suspicious group behavior in a poorly supervised part of the school building. While the situation is analyzed as if it were found in a secondary school, the discussion in many places is also pertinent to elementary schools.

> My classroom is at the far end of the building, away from the main administrative offices and most of the other teachers' rooms. While I keep my classroom door locked during the day and venture out only for snack supervision and lunch, I know that students congregate down at the end of the hall and at the fence not far from my classroom. I've mentioned the situation to the vice-principal and he agreed to patrol the area. But soon after he leaves the students are back again. I just know they are involved with drugs when they get together. Other teachers know of the drug problem on campus, but they seem to be able to ignore it better than I can.

## Social Literacy Training

| | |
|---|---|
| Key: | Open communications |
| Slogan: | "Speak true words about central conflicts" |
| Central Assumptions: | Classrooms provide few opportunities for open, honest communications |
| Goals: | "No-lose" conflict resolution |
| Important Aspects: | Consciousness-raising activities designed to reveal student and teacher concerns |

| | |
|---|---|
| | Teachers share responsibility for resolving conflicts with students |
| Potential Problems: | Problem resolution can be time-consuming |
| | The process is unsuited to on-the-spot intervention |
| | Some students may not take conflict-resolution "games" seriously |

## Systematic Management Plan for School Discipline

| | |
|---|---|
| Key: | Organizational change |
| Central Assumptions: | Problems are endemic to schools |
| | Organizational factors determine behavior |
| | Comprehensive — not piecemeal — change |
| Goals: | Address student behavior on a schoolwide basis |
| | Establish organizational mechanisms for reducing problems |
| Important Aspects: | Understanding the school as a rule-governed organization |
| | Data collection |
| | Conflict resolution |
| | Team troubleshooting |
| | Parental involvement |
| | Reinforcing environments for learning |
| | Professional development |
| Potential Problems: | The plan requires careful coordination |
| | It can be time-consuming |
| | Commitment of resources may be necessary |

# Social Literacy

---

## Key Questions

*The questions are intended to be asked by both teachers and students.*

1. *What is the problem?*
2. *Is the problem located in individuals or in rules and roles?*
3. *Have any changes in classroom or school organization been considered?*
4. *Is the problem-solving process democratic?*
5. *Is the solution mutually agreeable and satisfying?*

---

*What is the problem?* A teacher has grown increasingly more worried about what she perceives to be a growing drug problem at her school. Fearing for her safety and that of her students, she seeks administrative assistance but observes that periodic forays by the vice-principal do not put an end to student gatherings near her room. Part of her concern is based on the anxiety of never knowing when these gatherings might get "out of hand," producing a situation she cannot control.

Utilizing one of the activities central to Social Literacy Training, the teacher engages in "nuclear problem solving" with her colleagues. The first phase seeks to determine whether others share her perception of the problem. She discovers that many of her fellow teachers also are concerned about drug use on campus, particularly where younger students are becoming involved.

*Is the problem located in individuals or in rules and roles?* The second step in nuclear problem solving tries to identify patterns in student drug activity. Questions are raised about when students congregate and whether the same students are always involved. Teachers in other parts of the school comment on activities of a suspicious nature in their vicinity.

*Have any changes in classroom or school organization been considered?* According to Alfred Alschuler, "Socially literate solutions to discipline problems blame the system and change it rather than blaming individuals and attempting to change them."[8] The

---

[8] Alfred Alschuler, *School Discipline: A Socially Literate Solution* (New York: McGraw-Hill, 1980), p. 111.

teacher and her colleagues attempt to follow Alschuler's advice by brainstorming alternatives—alternative school rules, ways of organizing the school, and conceptions of roles. This third step of the problem-solving process is designed to generate as many alternatives as possible without evaluating them carefully. Some of the alternatives include:

1. Step up administrative supervision of areas where students tend to congregate.
2. Planning a series of on-campus workshops on the potential hazards of habitual drug use.
3. Providing pleasant locations (with music) for students to congregate at snack-break and lunch times.
4. Initiating "Friday Forums" at which students and teachers alike can comment on school concerns and suggest improvements.

The group members evaluate all the suggestions and select one to try.

*Is the problem-solving process democratic?* At this stage of the problem-solving process, Alschuler introduces a checklist by which group members can determine if their ways of using the Social Literacy approach permitted all participants to express their feelings. Other relevant role groups—students and parents, for example—may be invited at this point to participate in the problem-solving process, since they are affected by any decisions that will be made.

*Is the solution mutually agreeable and satisfying?* The Social Literacy Training three-step problem-solving process is a process, not a solution. In the present instance, the process has yielded a variety of alternatives, all of which have been examined and evaluated by teachers, students, and parents. One alternative is selected for trial. The teachers now engage in what Alschuler terms "democratic collaboration" in order to make plans for implementing the alternative they have chosen. Group members assign each other tasks and agree to keep one another informed of their progress. At the end of the process, our teacher feels pleased that her colleagues have taken her problem seriously and participated actively in the discussions. They decide to begin a series of Friday Forums to discuss the issues raised during nuclear problem solving with their students. Each teacher agrees to devote one class period of every class in the next week to open discussion of drug use on campus using the nuclear problem-solving process. A follow-up faculty meeting is scheduled in a week for information sharing and continued planning for ways to enhance teacher-student dialogue on these issues.

It is entirely possible that a long-term solution to campus drug problems will not emerge from these meetings, but at least our teacher no longer feels isolated from her colleagues. By sharing her concerns with colleagues, she discovered she was not alone. Other teachers were willing to work together in cooperative problem solving. Another group of faculty members might not prove as receptive to a single teacher's view of campus problems. Understanding the campus climate for airing problems and dealing with them constructively is necessary before an individual teacher is advised to utilize Social Literacy methods.

## *Systematic Management Plan for School Discipline (SMPSD)*

---

### Key Questions

1. *Does this behavior problem occur frequently?*
2. *If the problem is chronic, under what circumstances does it occur?*
3. *Are there any characteristics of classroom or school organization that might contribute to the problem?*
4. *In what ways can the problem be addressed on a comprehensive schoolwide basis?*

---

*Does this behavior problem occur frequently?* Students congregate in poorly supervised areas of the campus on a daily basis. Based on student comments and the smell of marijuana, it is apparent that part of the activities of these gatherings involves drug use.

*If the problem is chronic, under what circumstances does it occur?* Students do not have a place on campus that is officially designated as their "space." This fact probably leads them to identify out-of-the-way areas as rendezvous points. Students disperse whenever a teacher or administrator comes near, and constant supervision of isolated parts of the campus is difficult, given the busy schedules of most adults and the reluctance of many to risk student reprisals by intervening.

*Are there any characteristics of classroom or school organization that might contribute to the problem?* An analysis of the problem by teachers, administrators, and students does not focus directly on the issue of drug use, but instead concentrates on what circumstances facilitate student drug use. One factor is the absence of designated student lounges and gathering places located in the main part of the campus. Students are prompted to look for places they can call their own. These sites usually are situated in isolated areas, where it is easier to engage in use of controlled substances.

A second factor is the very existence of isolated parts of the campus. Teachers tend to undertake most activities within the four walls of their classrooms. Little instructional use is made of corridors and school grounds. Greater use of these areas during all parts of the day would make them less attractive places for students to congregate for illicit purposes.

A third factor concerns the nature of adult supervision of the campus. Administrators often are unable to cover the campus in a systematic manner. Individual teachers do not like to confront a group of students in an isolated part of the school. No coordinated plan for continuous campus supervision exists at present.

*In what ways can the problem be addressed on a comprehensive, schoolwide basis?* The first step is for the individuals who are expected to enforce school rules to meet and develop a well-coordinated plan for campus supervision. These people may include students, parent volunteers, and custodians as well as teachers and administrators. To prevent an individual "on patrol" from encountering a situation he or she cannot handle, supervision should be undertaken in teams of two or three. In this way, one person always is available to summon assistance.

The plan also should provide ideas concerning how to use isolated parts of the campus for instructional purposes. Learning stations can be set up in corridors. During good weather some classes can be held outside. Students can be helpful in determining how best to utilize these areas.

Finally, a room or area in a central location should be designated as a student conversation center. An effort should be made to create as pleasant an environment as possible. For example, a juke box and food machines can be provided. Students can use this facility as long as they are not engaged in proscribed activities. Individuals caught using drugs in the student center would lose the privilege of using it and be placed in a supervised detention room.

## Comparing Approaches

The preceding discussion focused on drug problems involving groups of students. In such cases, approaches employing school-wide planning and group problem-solving techniques seem particularly useful. The SPARK Program in New York City epitomizes a comprehensive effort to deal with drug problems. SPARK includes "counseling, home visits, parent workshops, parent-child group sessions, community involvement, curriculum development, the development of alternative activities to replace drugs and in-service training for teachers."[9] SPARK represents the kind of multifaceted approach characteristic of both Social Literacy Training and the SMPSD.

Logical Consequences, Positive Peer Culture, and Reality Therapy also emphasize the value of group problem solving but at a different organizational level — namely, the classroom or small group in which the focus might be on a single student's drug problems. Logical Consequences may encourage the discussion of the consequences of intensive drug misuse and provide opportunities for students to propose their own solutions to the problem. Rather than focusing on drug education per se, Reality Therapy may consider drug use a symptom, particularly in cases where students have experienced little academic or social success at school. Students would be encouraged to take a measure of responsibility in searching for solutions.

Positive Peer Culture places even more responsibility on students to help one another with their concerns. Once a student has brought a drug-related issue to the group meeting, participants brainstorm ways to deal with the concern. Peer influence has been demonstrated to be particularly effective in drug education programs.[10] One such program, the TRENDS (Teens React–En-

---

9 Richard H. Blum, *Drug Education: Results and Recommendations* (Lexington, Mass.: D.C. Heath and Company, 1976), p. 55.

10 ERS, Inc. "Drug Education: Goals, Approaches, Evaluation" (Educational Research Service, Inc., 1975).

courage New Directions for Savannah) Program in Savannah-Chatham County, Georgia, provides information on drugs, alcohol, smoking and venereal disease.[11] For this program, high school students are trained by community resource persons and then dispatched to elementary schools where they meet weekly with classes of sixth-grade students and provide instruction for a period of eight weeks. The forementioned SPARK Program in New York City also trains peers to serve as group leaders in counseling sessions.

Group problem solving is not necessarily a feature of TET, although a teacher might spend class time discussing ways to improve teacher-student communication in class and on campus. If students feel alienated from adults on campus, increased drug use might be one reaction. Since the question of "who owns the problem" is central to TET, a teacher must decide if drug use is the student's problem or the teacher's problem or if it affects them both. If the problem is primarily the student's, the teacher may refer the student to the appropriate community agency for help. If the problem affects both student and teacher, then collaborative problem solving and discussion are a better way to proceed.

While this chapter focuses on groups of students, it is possible to conceptualize such problems as smoking, drinking, and drug use as individual concerns. In such cases, Transactional Analysis, Behavior Modification, and Assertive Discipline may be appropriate. Behavior Modification, for example, has proven particularly successful with problems of addiction or drug habituation. The solutions, however, sometimes can be extreme and beyond the scope of school intervention — such as giving medication which induces vomiting or severe nausea immediately after ingestion of alcohol or drugs and therapies in which patients are forced to satiate themselves with the addictive substance until they can no longer bear the sight of it. The extent to which most teachers are able to employ Behavior Modification probably will be limited to reinforcement of students when they are not using controlled substances and withdrawal of privileges when they do.

The sort of personal counseling used in Transactional Analysis may be helpful in some instances where misuse of controlled substances has not become too serious. If a student's drug use creates problems in class, a teacher may arrange to conference privately

11 Educational Research Service, Inc., p. 40.

with the student to explain what he has observed and how student behavior interferes with his schoolwork and the teacher-student relationship. The success of clinical contacts may depend on the strength of the teacher's relationship with the student prior to the conference. The focus in TA is on the student's need to communicate effectively with adults and to develop self-esteem, rather than on drug issues per se.

The teacher utilizing Assertive Discipline techniques is not trained specifically to deal with drug issues. The "severe clause" which requires the student to immediately leave the classroom may be used in cases involving drug possession or intoxication. The problem would then be handled outside class by an administrator, parents, and local authorities.

## Activities

1. Ask students to identify resource persons in the community adjacent to your school who are particularly helpful in assisting young people with personal concerns. Share this list of resource people with colleagues and administrators.
2. Determine which are the best community referral agencies in your area for dealing with student alcoholism and drug abuse. Contact each of the referral agencies and identify a key resource person. Compile a list of these resources for use in making student referrals.
3. Do you know what to look for in determining whether or not a student has been drinking or using drugs? List the physical signs associated with use of the following: alcohol, marijuana, amphetamines, and barbiturates.
4. Problems related to student drug use can involve a variety of legal issues. Laws vary from state to state. Find out your rights and responsibilities related to the following: searching a student's person for drugs, searching a student's locker for drugs, reporting a student possessing drugs to the police, and reporting a student "high" on drugs to the police.

# FIGHTING AND AGGRESSIVE BEHAVIOR PROBLEMS

Perhaps the most frightening of student behavior problems, fighting and physically aggressive acts combine the qualities of a problem to be understood with the urgency of a potentially dangerous situation. Erupting suddenly, acts of aggression allow little time for reflection and deliberation. Teachers who intervene to stop fighting often risk their own safety to do so.

Students, too, worry about their physical safety in school. The Safe Schools Study estimates that 280,000 secondary students are attacked in school every month.[1] With the growth of local youth gangs, students are under increasing peer pressure to involve themselves in aggressive acts. In many communities today students stand a greater risk of being victimized in school than away from school. No longer are schools sanctuaries from the violence of the outside world.

Besides the threat to physical safety, fighting and other acts of aggression interrupt classroom activities. During a fight, the combatants and often their audience are out of control. It is impossible to teach until order has been restored. Even after the fight has been stopped, it may not be easy to get back to "business as usual." Students who have observed the fighting are unsettled and frequently want to talk about the incident, its causes, and likely consequences. It is difficult to resume planned activities for the day, and valuable teaching-learning time is lost.

Teachers are often distressed when students appear to waste time fighting over what seem to be trivial matters. Jane and Susie

---

[1] National Institute of Education, *Violent Schools — Safe Schools*, The Safe School Study Report to the Congress. Vol. I (Washington, D.C.: National Institute of Education, 1978).

begin screaming and pulling one another's hair because Jane called Susie an unflattering name; Sam and Danny engage in a brawl because Sam used Danny's comb in the P.E. locker room; elementary-age students begin fighting after a game of shoving gets out of hand. Because these are problems between students, researchers tend to overlook them.[2] For their part educators tend to enforce those rules that exist for their own protection and convenience, rather than that of their students! Students learn quickly that their own problems — name calling, fighting, extortion, and theft of personal property — typically are of secondary importance to the adults at school.

What to do with acts of aggression is not widely agreed upon. Should students be automatically suspended from school and given a chance to "cool off"? Should students be taught peaceful ways to resolve conflicts between one another? Should classroom time be given over to discussion of school fighting? Should all of the above be incorporated into schoolwide plans for making campuses safe places for students and teachers alike?

Current practices for documenting fights are so unsystematic that little useful information is available from school officials. The aftermath of fighting is not well recorded. One reason is that fights are sudden occurrences and teachers rarely have time or are required to write out disciplinary referrals explaining what happened or suggesting what to do with combatants. Another reason for sketchy documentation is that it is not always easy to determine who actually starts a fight. Was it the student who threw the first punch or the one who called the name?

# HANDLING AN IN-CLASS FIGHT

Each of the nine approaches to classroom management suggests some ways to deal with aggressive student behaviors. Behavior Modification (pp. 88–90) and Transactional Analysis (pp. 90–92) are highlighted in this chapter because they offer suggestions that seem particularly useful for individual students. While the focus is on the aftermath of a hypothetical fighting incident, it is our assumption that the teacher's first responsibility is to prevent stu-

---

2 Daniel L. Duke, "Adults Can Be Discipline Problems Too!" *Psychology in the Schools*, Vol. 15, no. 4 (October 1978), p. 527.

dents from injuring one another. Teachers are advised to prepare contingency plans for how to handle fights anywhere on campus. Formulating a plan of action in advance often can spell the difference between control and chaos. What to do once the fighting has stopped is a matter for discussion; stopping the fight is not.

The incident to be discussed in this chapter takes place in an elementary class, but the situation certainly can be found in secondary schools as well. With some students, teachers may be physically unable to break up a fight alone. Knowing who can be called on for assistance is probably the first course of action for any teacher.

> I was scared. When Paul and Sam started fighting near the pencil sharpener in the back of the room, all I could see was arms and legs, ripped clothing, and broken pencils being used as weapons. The fury with which those boys were attacking each other paralyzed me for a moment, but I took a quick breath and walked toward them. At the same time, I asked one of the other students to run to the office and bring back the vice-principal. As I moved toward the boys, my feelings of fear changed to anger — anger in particular at Paul, who started the brawl. He has become a real troublemaker.

As a refresher, the major aspects of Behavior Modification and Transactional Analysis are summarized below.

| Behavior Modification | |
|---|---|
| Key: | Reinforcement |
| Central Assumptions: | Students misbehave because the consequences of misbehavior are reinforcing |
| Goals: | Decrease negative behavior |
| | Increase positive behavior |
| Important Aspects: | Rewarding desirable behavior is more effective than punishing undesirable behavior |

| | |
|---|---|
| | Ignore attention-seeking misconduct |
| | Avoid expecting dramatic changes in behavior |
| Potential Problems: | Not all misbehavior may be attention seeking |
| | Behavior Modification overlooks an understanding of the root causes of behavior problems |
| | Finding adequate reinforcers for older students may be difficult |

## Transactional Analysis

| | |
|---|---|
| Key: | Interpersonal communications |
| Central Assumptions: | People have three ego states: child, parent, and adult |
| | Problems arise when people interact on basis of different ego states |
| Goal: | Understand the gamelike nature of communications |
| Important Aspects: | Clinical contacts between teacher and student |
| | Active listening |
| | Awareness of origins of behavior |
| Potential Problems: | The process can be time-consuming |
| | Teachers may feel discomfort in a "clinical" role |
| | Potential harm if follow-up is not provided |

# Behavior Modification

## Key Questions

1. *What is the specific behavior that requires modification (elimination, reduction, increase)?*
2. *When does the behavior occur?*
3. *What are the immediate consequences of this behavior? In other words, what occurs in the classroom when a student manifests this behavior?*
4. *How can these consequences serve to reinforce the inappropriate behavior?*
5. *How can the consequences be altered?*
6. *How can appropriate behavior be reinforced in the future?*

*What is the specific behavior that requires modification in this case?* Paul's teacher already seems to have concluded that he is the aggressor. If she were to be as fair as possible, however, she would review the events of the preceding days. Before a decision can be made about whose behavior needs modifying, further information on the frequency of fighting for each boy is needed. Paul's teacher recalls that he has been involved in three other fights within the past month — two in her classroom and one in the cafeteria. On each occasion, Paul fought with a different boy. Sam, on the other hand, has not been involved in fighting since the beginning of school.

After determining that Paul has engaged in fighting more often than Sam, the teacher talks with each boy about the current incident. She decides that Paul initiated the fight by calling Sam names and pushing him away from the pencil sharpener. Paul claims that his action was warranted, however, because Sam had insulted him earlier in the day. In Paul's words, "Sam got what he deserved!"

Ms. Taylor would like to reduce the frequency of Paul's fighting behavior, but she is uncertain about the best way to proceed. She also worries about "Paul's attitude problems." Paul insists his actions were justified. He neglects the fact that Sam had made a simple request, in return for which he was pushed away from the pencil sharpener. Further data is needed before Ms. Taylor can map out a Behavior Modification program.

*When does the behavior occur?* At first, it appears that there are no patterns to Paul's fighting. However, after discussing Paul's behavior with a teacher who observed his cafeteria fight, the teacher realizes that all of Paul's fights actually take place about the same time of day. On each occasion, Paul involved himself in a fight between 10:15 and 10:30, during or immediately after the morning snack break.

*What are the immediate consequences of Paul's behavior? In other words, what occurs when Paul acts aggressively?* The teacher remembers that when Paul began fighting with Sam in her classroom, two of his friends ran back to the fight scene and cheered him on with encouraging comments. At the time she took little notice of their actions, except to be distressed by their conduct.

*How can these consequences serve to reinforce the inappropriate behavior?* Paul's two friends are slightly older and larger boys. They are leaders in their age group and admired by many of the students. Paul may be seeking their approval and recognition by engaging in behavior which they support. Indeed, Paul's music teacher reports that one of these boys is a student in the music class where Paul fought recently. The music teacher also observes that Paul walks around campus with the two older boys. Paul's fighting behavior may be directed at earning their respect.

*How can the consequences be altered?* Deciding that Paul's behavior is influenced by the external positive reinforcement provided by his two older friends, the teacher talks with the pair to determine if they will cooperate in reducing Paul's aggressive behavior. The two boys do not seem very cooperative. She asks them if they would consent to be switched to another class for a two-week trial period, and they agree.

During the next two weeks, Paul's teacher reinforces Paul each day he does not engage in fighting by giving him bonus points. At the end of each week, he can exchange the points for a reward. Paul helps determine what the reward will be. He and his teacher agree that if he avoids fighting for five days in a row he will be able to use the art room for the last hour of the day on Friday.

*How can appropriate behavior be reinforced in the future?* Paul's teacher devises a schedule for gradually increasing the number of days that Paul must avoid fighting in order to earn a prize. In addition, she contacts his music, art, and physical education teachers to enlist their cooperation. They agree to reinforce Paul when he refrains from fighting and to report to her any instances of aggressive behavior. Finally, Paul's teacher meets periodically with him to discuss nonaggressive ways to deal with frustrating and troublesome situations. A key component of this training is learning to express discontent verbally.

## Transactional Analysis

Transactional Analysis represents an approach quite distinct from Behavior Modification. Little emphasis is placed on reinforcement schedules. The following questions may be asked by a teacher employing TA to deal with Paul's fighting.

---

### Key Questions

1. *What is the behavior that I find troublesome?*
2. *Has this behavior occurred before?*
3. *What is the ego state of the student when he behaves this way and what is my ego state when I respond?*
4. *What is the gamelike nature of our interaction?*
5. *How can I communicate my perceptions to the student?*

---

*What is the behavior that is troublesome?* In order to deal with Paul's fighting behavior using T.A., Paul's teacher needs information not provided in the original description of the problem. Specifically, she needs to study her own behavior in response to Paul and Sam's fighting. Instead of focusing only on Paul's behavior, T.A. assumes that something else is going on besides the obvious transactions.

*Has this behavior occurred before?* Reviewing the incidents in her classroom, the teacher remembers that she handled the aftermath of the previous fights in the same way. Each time, she took Paul and the other student aside and questioned them about their behavior. The exchange between the students and her went something like this:

Teacher:    "All right, boys. Tell me what happened."
Paul:       "Sam called me names on the bus this morning and then he tried to steal my pencil just now."

Sam:       "It's my pencil. He's lying to you!"
Teacher:   "Now calm down, you two! I'm trying to hear both
           sides of this."

*What are the ego states of the students when they behave this way and what is the teacher's ego state when she responds?* In order to understand the nature of communications between individuals, T.A. proponents identify interactions in terms of parent, adult, and child ego states and draw simple diagrams describing them. The preceding exchange between the teacher, Paul, and Sam can be depicted in the following manner:

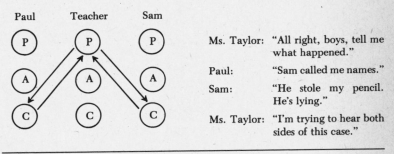

Ms. Taylor: "All right, boys, tell me what happened."

Paul:       "Sam called me names."

Sam:        "He stole my pencil. He's lying."

Ms. Taylor: "I'm trying to hear both sides of this case."

*Figure 6-1*

According to T.A. theory, the most appropriate teacher ego state is the adult ego state. Therefore, the parent-child interaction depicted in the diagram would be considered dysfunctional. In order to improve the situation, further information is needed about teacher-student communication.

*What is the gamelike nature of the interaction?* A review of *Games Students Play* by T.A. analyst Ken Ernst reveals that the kind of exchange described above represents a set of games known as "I Know Best" teacher games.[3] Specifically labeled the "courtroom game," the interaction calls for the teacher to act as judge and jury by interrogating the students involved in the "crime." As judge and jury, the teacher determines who is "guilty" and what the punishments should be. Paul and Sam have no part in resolving the difficulties between them when the courtroom game is played.

---

[3] The use of the term "game" does not usually imply enjoyment to T.A. analysts. By definition, a game is a "recurring set of transactions, often repetitious, superficially plausible, with a concealed motivation; or, more colloquially a series of moves with a snare, or 'gimmick.' " Eric Berne, *Games People Play*, p. 84.

*How can the teacher communicate her perceptions to the students?* The first person needing insight into the transaction is the teacher. She must realize that her habit of behaving like a parent and unilaterally resolving student problems may discourage students from working toward handling their own problems in an adultlike manner. Next, she must communicate these perceptions to the students. Once the communication pattern is understood by all participants, the teacher declares that she will not intervene in problems that Paul and Sam should solve on their own, unless others are affected.

T.A. assumes that once the teacher and her students begin to communicate straightforwardly about what is really going on in the classroom, there will be less need for game playing. It is the teacher's responsibility to recognize classroom games, reveal nonproductive patterns to the students, and encourage more honest communication.

## Comparing Approaches

Behavior Modification and Transactional Analysis embody two quite distinct approaches to fighting behavior. Yet both reflect the view that students behave inappropriately because the consequences of their behaviors are reinforcing, no matter whether the behaviors are learned (as in Behavior Modification) or are a reflection of an ego state (as in Transactional Analysis). The two approaches provide teachers with different "solutions" as well. In the case of Behavior Modification, the teacher determines that peer attention is the reinforcing consequence of Paul's fighting; in the T.A. version, the teacher's attention serves to reinforce Paul and Sam's behavior. In certain instances, it is conceivable that both interpretations of the causes of fighting are correct and that both solutions need to be implemented.

Behavior Modification can work well when a single student's behavior needs to be altered. Group behavior, such as gang-initiated fighting, is not handled as well with Behavior Modification because the reinforcing consequences for negative behavior vary widely among students. Changing a given reinforcer may affect certain students' behaviors in the group but is unlikely to change the group's behavior. Group reinforcers can be successful, however, in controlling individual student's behavior. Campbell, Adams, and Ryabik (1974) describe a group contingency program used to control fighting and encourage correct postures for students riding on a school bus.[4] They employed the following group contingency successfully: following any fighting, the bus stopped for a period of twenty seconds. This time-out procedure effectively eliminated fighting.

Dreikurs' Logical Consequences is perhaps the closest of the other approaches to T.A., in that it stresses making students (and teachers) aware of their behavior and its impact on others.[5] Dreikurs, however, would recommend that students be involved in the initial determination of a corrective course of action. T.A. calls on the teacher to determine what the problem is and what the solution will be. Teacher Effectiveness Training also encourages student involvement in problem analysis and solution generation. TET focuses on the quality of teacher-student communication even more than does Transactional Analysis. Gordon actually specifies pronouns and phrases to avoid when the objective is productive communication.

Assertive Discipline, on the other hand, is more like Behavior Modification, in that it focuses on eliminating classroom fighting rather than understanding it first. Fighting is usually an automatic suspension from class. Students cannot return to class until a parent-teacher conference and thirty minutes of detention have been completed.

Positive Peer Culture, Social Literacy Training, and Reality Therapy all treat fighting as an appropriate topic for group discussion and intervention. Glasser might also examine Paul's academic work and determine if his fighting is in part a reaction to his frustration in failing to meet teacher expectations for schoolwork. Social Literacy Training and the SMPSD might use Paul's case as an opportunity to take a general look at the causes for fighting. These two approaches do not assume that all behavior problems are based on student, teacher, or teacher-student characteristics. They acknowledge the possibility that schools and classrooms may be organized in ways that encourage aggressive behavior. For example, fighting at the pencil sharpener may be

---

4 William R. Jensen, "Behavior Modification in Secondary Schools: A Review," *Journal of Research and Development in Education*, Vol. 11, no. 5 (Summer 1978), p. 60.

5 In fact, Ken Ernst in *Games Students Play* makes reference to Dreikurs' use of the "bathroom technique" when dealing with two siblings who are arguing. The parent goes into the bathroom, locks the door, and waits until the siblings have completed the argument, leaving them to deal with their own problems.

controlled "organizationally by allowing only one student at a time to sharpen his pencil.

The example discussed in this chapter involved fighting between elementary-age students. Obviously, fighting among older students can be a more serious problem, since they are capable of inflicting greater injury and less likely to yield to teacher intervention. While many of the principles on which the approaches are based are pertinent to secondary-school students, teachers are advised to get assistance whenever possible to stop a fight. Once the fighting has ceased, an approach can be implemented to reduce the likelihood it will occur again.

## Activities

1. Ask three experienced colleagues how they handled student fighting in the past. Discuss their responses in light of the approaches in this chapter.
2. Contact a local law enforcement officer and ask him how he is trained to handle fights without using weapons. Are any of his techniques applicable to school situations?
3. The example discussed in the chapter involved elementary-age students. What changes might have to be made if Behavior Modification or Transactional Analysis were used with older students?
4. Prepare a set of "contingency plans" for getting help from other teachers or administrators in the event a serious fight breaks out—in class, in the hall, and on campus. Ask several students to evaluate the plans and try to suggest improvements.

# STUDENT DISRESPECT
# TOWARD OTHER STUDENTS

The complaint is all too familiar. "Young people have no respect these days." Those uttering such words generally are adults. Adults represent authority, particularly in organizational settings like schools. Any act by a student which challenges this authority or the persons responsible for exercising it can be interpreted as a potential threat, not only to the particular individuals involved but, in many cases, to the entire enterprise of schooling.

Adults, however, often overlook the fact that disrespect also can characterize interactions among peers. In fact, it is likely that instances of student disrespect toward other students are more numerous than those between students and teachers. Incidents between students, however, rarely get much publicity. They are not reported in a systematic fashion. Therefore it is easy to underestimate the seriousness of student disrespect toward other students.

Students are likely to be as concerned about behavior problems as are teachers. And with good reason. The Safe School Study reported that adolescents today stand a greater chance of being victimized at school than off campus.[1] In particular students worry about theft, personal safety, and extortion. They also are concerned about verbal abuse, embarrassment, intimidation, and humiliation. These problems can have a substantial negative impact on the school experience of many students — leading some to avoid school altogether. It goes without saying that the more threatening the school environment is for students, the less likely they are to come to school or to apply themselves when in school.

---

[1] National Institute of Education, *Violent Schools — Safe Schools*, The Safe School Study Report to the Congress, Vol. I (Washington, D.C.: National Institute of Education, 1978).

For our purposes disrespect will be defined as any behavior (or refusal to exhibit behavior) that is intended to interfere with the normal conduct of activities by another person. We thus consider disrespect to encompass a broad range of specific behavior problems, including criminal acts such as theft, impoliteness, defamatory remarks, and racial slurs. Disrespect does not include "victimless" problems such as truancy or smoking, where, in most cases, only the perpetrator is adversely affected.

In thinking about disrespect, it is useful to consider two dimensions—intentionality and perception.[2] Intentionality refers to the desire of a given individual to commit a disrespectful act. Perception pertains to whether or not the act is perceived as disrespectful. Figure 7-1 depicts the four possible combinations of these dimensions.

| | | **Perception** | |
|---|---|---|---|
| | | Behavior perceived to be disrespectful | Behavior not perceived to be disrespectful |
| **Intentionality** | Behavior intended to be disrespectful | 1 | 2 |
| | Behavior not intended to be disrespectful | 3 | 4 |

*Figure 7-1 Dimensions of Disrespect*

In thinking about behavior problems, it is important to remember that a problem is not a problem until it is identified as such. At the point, therefore, when a student calls out to his teacher using the teacher's first name, the teacher must decide whether this behavior constitutes a problem or not. The teacher may perceive the remark as disrespectful, even though that was not the student's intention (3). Or the teacher may not perceive the remark to be disrespectful, though it was intended as such (2). In either case, the teacher's misperception may actually create a problem. In the case of the former, the student may feel falsely accused. In the latter instance, he may believe that he has "put one over on the teacher," a belief that can spawn further disrespectful behavior.

[2] Our thanks to William Moon of Stanford University for assistance in conceptualizing disrespect.

# HANDLING STUDENT DISRESPECT TOWARD OTHER STUDENTS

Dealing with disrespect can be one of the trickiest and most perplexing classroom management problems for teachers. Various ways to handle disrespect are covered by the nine approaches in this book. In this chapter we highlight Positive Peer Culture and the Systematic Management Plan for School Discipline, seeing how each can be employed to reduce the likelihood that students will exhibit little respect for each other. These two approaches were selected because they both try to create opportunities for students to help each other, but each entails somewhat different modifications of classroom organization. PPC emphasizes creating forums in which students can listen to each other's problems. The SMPSD focuses on classroom goals and reward structure.

The problem to be addressed by PPC and the SMPSD takes place in a recently desegregated middle school. Similar problems, though, can also be found in elementary and high schools where students from different backgrounds are brought together as a result of court order or governmental action.

> Ever since the fall when the new desegregation plan was implemented, my sixth-grade class has been chaotic. I've never worked with such unruly kids before — black or white. Black kids taunt white kids. White kids taunt black kids. They call each other names. They steal each other's lunches and books. I never feel I'm in control, even on the best of days. It's like sitting on a powder keg. I've never worked with inner-city students before, but I'm a good teacher. Maybe I'm getting too old, though. Ten years is a long time in the same school. If I just got more administrative support — or at least a teacher aide — maybe I could get down to teaching these kids. They sure need it. Most of them are below grade level in reading and math.

There follow synopses of Positive Peer Culture and the Systematic Management Plan for School Discipline.

## Positive Peer Culture

| | |
|---|---|
| Key: | Peer support |
| Central Assumptions: | Problems are normal |
| | Troubled students can help themselves by first helping others |

| Goal: | Provide opportunities for students to help each other |
|---|---|
| Important Aspects: | Single-sex groups of nine troubled students and one adult leader |
| | New members spend first meetings working on others' problems |
| | Each meeting focuses on one student's concerns |
| Potential Problems: | The process is time consuming |
| | It is unsuited to on-the-spot intervention |
| | Group leaders must make a long-term commitment |

## Systematic Management Plan for School Discipline

| Key: | Organizational change |
|---|---|
| Central Assumptions: | Problems are endemic to schools |
| | Organizational factors determine behavior |
| | Comprehensive — not piecemeal — change |
| Goals: | Address student behavior on a schoolwide basis |
| | Establish organizational mechanisms for reducing problems |
| Important Aspects: | Understanding the school as a rule-governed organization |
| | Data collection |
| | Conflict resolution |
| | Team troubleshooting |
| | Parental involvement |

|  | Reinforcing environments for learning |
|---|---|
|  | Professional development |
| Potential Problems: | The technique requires careful coordination |
|  | It is time-consuming |
|  | Commitment of resources may be necessary |

## *Positive Peer Culture*

### Key Questions

1. *What are my expectations regarding how students relate to each other?*
2. *Can I begin to regard student problems as opportunities to help students learn responsibility and caring?*
3. *Can I find time to operate peer meetings or can I encourage others in the school to make these opportunities available?*
4. *Are there ways in which I can encourage students to help each other instead of relying on me or another adult?*

*What are my expectations regarding how students relate to each other?* The opening vignette differs from those in previous chapters in that it concerns the behavior of an entire class. For this reason, PPC seems particularly appropriate. The key questions for PPC differ from most of the key questions for other approaches. They are more general and focus more on teacher expectations and assumptions than do the other sets of questions. They also are not tied to any specific problem but instead to the feasibility of implementing a particular problem-solving process.

Let us call our sixth-grade teacher Cheryl. With ten years of elementary school experience, she has had ample time to develop a variety of expectations about how students behave. She has never experienced behavior problems on a widespread basis before, so she basically has felt that her classroom management skills were adequate—until now. Confronted with collective student disrespect toward each other, she is forced to reflect on what she believes about students.

Cheryl thinks that sixth graders are beginning to develop adolescent identities. She realizes that part of this process entails challenging adult authority. In the past, she has noticed cliques forming, but they generally have not been antagonistic toward each other. Cheryl cannot help but attribute the recent change in student behavior to changes in the racial composition of her classroom. With half the class now made up of black students, she began the school year expecting friction between blacks and whites to occur. In fact, she admits that this expectation predated actual school desegregation and represented a reason why she opposed it.

While Cheryl's beliefs about the inevitability of disharmony between black and white students would interfere with her adoption of PPC, the fact that she also feels sixth graders share a common developmental experience—the establishment of individual identities through grouping—can be useful. Nowhere in her thinking is there the notion that students are incapable of helping each other. At the same time, Cheryl has grown to expect herself to be the one to resolve classroom problems when they arise. She must learn to accept the fact that students often may be better resolvers of classroom problems—particularly ones they create—than she. It has become easier for Cheryl to accept this fact now that all of her attempts to create harmony in this year's class have failed.

*Can Cheryl begin to regard student problems as opportunities to help students learn responsibility and caring?* This question forces Cheryl to go beyond the preceding painful admission that her students may be more effective classroom managers in certain situations than she. It concerns whether or not Cheryl is prepared to redefine behaviors she once considered to be problems as opportunities instead.

There are costs associated with viewing problems as opportunities. For one thing, mechanisms already exist in most classes for dealing with problems. Thus, students who are disruptive or who are caught stealing are simply sent to the principal. If Cheryl decides that the tensions between black and white students instead constitute opportunities for the class to explore such important subjects as race relations, group dynamics, and stereotyping, she must pay a price in the extra time and energy required to shift the focus of her activities.

Potential benefits exist to offset the costs in terms of extra time and energy. These benefits include reducing the level of tension in class, increasing student understanding of complex social forces, developing student problem-solving skills, and encouraging students to assume responsibility for the consequences of their own behavior. Let us assume that Cheryl considers the situation and decides these potential benefits outweigh the costs of defining her current problem as an opportunity.

*Can Cheryl find time to operate peer meetings or can she encourage others in the school to make these opportunities available?* While most high schools have guidance counselors and other certificated personnel who are not scheduled into classes, middle and elementary schools typically have few such individuals. For this reason, Cheryl probably must initiate peer meetings herself. She should give serious consideration to involving another group facilitator — for example, a high school student, fellow teacher, the principal, a counselor, or a parent — only if she has reason to believe that the tension in class is in large part a function of students' dislike or distrust of her.

Finding time for unanticipated activities is always a challenge for teachers, who already tend to have more to do than available time permits. If we assume, however, that tensions are undermining the productivity of Cheryl's class, the time devoted to conflict reduction appears to be a justifiable investment.

A regular time for peer meetings must be scheduled, preferably on a daily basis. At first, students may not take the meetings seriously or they may test Cheryl to see how far she will go in sharing responsibility. By meeting regularly, students eventually may become accustomed to the routine and begin to view the opportunity to discuss their concerns as a fixed part of the day.

*Are there ways in which Cheryl can encourage students to help each other instead of relying on her or another adult?* Patience is the key, according to PPC. Students have been conditioned for years to look to the teacher for resolution of classroom conflicts. It takes time for them to readjust to the fact that Cheryl may not step in and try to handle every difficult situation. Cheryl must allow herself to tolerate considerable student frustration because students often try to give up after a few attempts at problem solving. Only when they see that Cheryl refuses to rescue them from a situation they have created will her students begin to grapple with the problem in earnest. At this point, Cheryl can offer alternative strategies or help move meetings along when they get "stuck," but her role is strictly that of a facilitator.

The major thrust of PPC is to provide young people with opportunities to help themselves while helping others. It is important for a young person to see that others need not always benefit at his expense. In the context of Cheryl's class, this means that peer meetings should look at the reasons why individual students behave the way they do—siding with peers of the same race, taunting students of a different race, stealing personal property. Cheryl should expect to intervene when necessary to keep the focus of discussion on the motives and concerns of individuals rather than groups of students.

Vorrath and Brendtro (1974) feel it is easier to work on problems with young people if the support groups are not coeducational. Obviously, it is easier to restrict groups by sex in residential treatment centers (where PPC got its start) than in public schools. It is possible, though, for Cheryl to divide the class into two groups—one for boys and the other for girls—and meet with one at a time. If she has a teacher aide or volunteer available, this person can work with one group while Cheryl works with the other, thus reducing the likelihood of one group growing restless while the other is meeting.

*The peer group in action.* It is pointless to describe how Cheryl's groups might deal with the tensions in class because no two classes or groups of students are alike. The PPC process is not intended to make all problem resolution uniform or compel young people to develop common responses to problems.

What Cheryl should expect to happen, however, is that students—slowly at first—will gain experience reporting their personal concerns with classroom issues to their peers—both black and white. Most students probably feel as uncomfortable as Cheryl with the tensions and behavior problems in class. At some level, they doubtless would like to eliminate the conflicts and get on with schoolwork. Group pride—in this case rooted in racial identities—is serving to inhibit either group from taking the first step toward conflict resolution. By having students talk only about their individual reactions to the tensions, PPC can defuse the potency of negative peer influence, so that the entire group (or class) can reconstitute itself as a helping body seeking to make class as productive and comfortable as possible.

Each PPC meeting is devoted to discussing the concerns of one student. Vorrath and Brendtro provide guidelines about how to decide which student. Some questions the group needs to address in this regard include:

1. Who seems to need the meeting most?
2. Who is in a position to use the meeting to best advantage?
3. How long since the person last was the focus of the meeting?
4. How hard is a person fighting to get the meeting?

In Cheryl's class, the group may decide that someone who has just been the victim of a racial slur or a theft needs group attention the most on a given day. The very process of deciding who to work with is designed to shift attention away from negative issues and group identities and toward the provision of assistance.

## Systematic Management Plan for School Discipline (SMPSD)

Positive Peer Culture is an approach requiring a relatively large investment of teacher time and complex arrangements concerning where and when to meet. Under certain circumstances it may be possible to accomplish similar objectives by modifying certain aspects of classroom organization. The SMPSD offers a variety of options for organizational improvements designed to reduce friction among students.

---

### Key Questions

1. *Does the problem occur frequently?*
2. *If the problem is chronic, under what circumstances does it occur?*
3. *Are there any characteristics of classroom or school organization that might contribute to the problem?*
4. *In what ways can the problem be addressed on a comprehensive basis?*

---

*Does the problem occur frequently?* From the initial description it appears that the friction between students occurs frequently enough to warrant consideration of possible ways in which classroom organization may be contributing to the problem.

*If the problem is chronic, under what circumstances does it occur?* Students in Cheryl's class exchange jibes and pick on each other primarily during times when large-group instruction is not taking place. Interestingly, Cheryl had reduced the amount of large-group instruction this year because of pressure from the administration to individualize instruction. School officials felt that the interests of students performing below grade level would be better served by individualized instruction. By increasing the occasions when students work on their own, this strategy tends to increase the likelihood that students will grow restless waiting for teacher assistance. Such times frequently are characterized by acts of student disrespect toward each other.

*Are there any characteristics of classroom or school organization that might contribute to the problem?* As mentioned in the preceding section, the use of individualized instruction diminishes the amount of direct teacher supervision and makes it easier for students to behave in a disrespectful manner. In addition, there are few formal opportunities in Cheryl's class when students are expected to help or cooperate with each other.

*In what ways can the problem be addressed on a comprehensive basis?* In light of the two comments above, Cheryl might be advised to reduce the amount of time that students engage in individual seatwork. Clear guidelines concerning student participation in classroom activities should be established, preferably with student input. Consequences for failure to abide by these guidelines also should be specified, again with students given an opportunity to contribute suggestions.

These strategies will help create a businesslike atmosphere in class. Such a climate can substantially reduce the number of unproductive incidents in Cheryl's class. However, it is unlikely to facilitate any changes in how students from different backgrounds feel about each other. To accomplish this more challenging task, it may be necessary to modify the basis on which rewards and praise in class are allocated.

Conventional classrooms are set up to reward the efforts of individuals. Such a system does not encourage students to cooperate with each other. What if Cheryl alters the basis on which grades on particular assignments are given? If she gave the entire class the same grade on certain assignments and if this grade represented the work of the lowest-achieving student in class, then it would be in the best interests of all her students to help each other as much as possible. Should only one student be left behind, the entire class would suffer.

The SMPSD is premised on the belief that organizational factors such as the reward structure and the way students are grouped for instruction exert considerable influence over how students behave. Changes that ignore these organizational factors often are condemned to failure.

## Comparing Approaches

It is not uncommon for busy educators to minimize the consequences of interpersonal problems for young people. Friction between students can disrupt instruction and undermine concentration, thus making the teacher's job more difficult. Left unresolved, problems involving students can lead to avoidance of school and development of serious psychological difficulties.

PPC, Reality Therapy, and SMPSD are based on the premise that students have personal concerns that deserve discussion and assistance in school. Social Literacy Training and TET also provide for open discussion of student concerns, but they tend to focus primarily on concerns that contribute to classroom management problems. All of the above approaches except the SMPSD specify guidelines for conducting problem-exploration sessions with students and all call on teachers to serve as facilitators rather than directive group leaders.

Faced with student disrespect for other students, educators utilizing Social Literacy Training and the SMPSD are likely to try and involve the entire school, rather than limiting the discussion to one classroom. These approaches assume that little can be done to ease major tensions without ensuring that all students and teachers in a school share a common awareness of the problem situation and have an equal opportunity to contribute to its resolution.

Social Literacy Training may try to engage teachers, administrators, and students in one of several "games" described by Alschuler. For example, to improve understanding of the circumstances surrounding racial tensions, groups of students and educators can participate in the nuclear problem-solving process, where individuals identify patterns of conflict and analyze aspects of school and classroom organization that contribute to tensions. As a result of undergoing this process, it may be discovered that tensions exist in part because there are too few structured activities requiring black and white students to cooperate in the attainment of desired objectives. Once causes of tension are identified, group members can participate in generating solutions.

Other approaches to classroom management — including Assertive Discipline, Behavior Modification, Logical Consequences, and Transactional Analysis — tend not to rely heavily on group process or on schoolwide and communitywide involvement. Were the teacher in our example to employ Assertive Discipline or Behavior Modification, she would deal primarily with the overt classroom behaviors resulting from racial tensions, rather than the origins of the tensions. In the case of Assertive Discipline, classroom rules would be developed and enforced consistently. Enforcing the rules can reduce outbursts, thefts, and other unproductive behaviors, but it is uncertain if underlying racial attitudes will be altered very much.

As for Behavior Modification, a teacher may try to introduce a reinforcement system that rewards students when they cooperate with each other and withholds rewards or employs punishments when they do not cooperate. Such systems can be operated on an individual or a group basis. One of the most interesting Behavior Modification strategies for dealing with classwide problems is the "Good Behavior Game." Developed for use in highly disruptive Los Angeles classes, the game calls for dividing classes into two groups. In Cheryl's case, the division might be done in such a way as to ensure that black and white students were evenly distributed among both groups. Groups compete for daily and weekly rewards as well as an annual reward in June. The rewards can be decided by the students themselves or by the teacher and need not be costly. Daily rewards go to the group with the fewest number of behavior problems. If one or two students consistently misbehave and ruin their group's chances of getting rewarded, these individuals need to be removed from the "Good Behavior Game" and handled separately.

Logical Consequences and Transactional Analysis are approaches more oriented to intervention with individual students than whole classes. Were Cheryl to employ either of these approaches she probably would look at each classroom incident separately, speaking individually with the students involved and questioning the motives behind their behavior. These two approaches obviously require a significant investment of time and energy when an entire class is disorderly. Group-oriented approaches may be more practical, though not necessarily more effective.

## Activities

1. The nine approaches to classroom management described in this book need not be mutually exclusive. Describe ways that Positive Peer Culture can be combined with other approaches to allow Cheryl to deal with the racial tension in her classroom.

2. Racial tension is one source of group tension. Another is based on the integration of students from different socioeconomic levels. Would you handle Cheryl's class any differently if tensions derived from the confrontation of working-class students and middle-class students?

3. List all the behaviors that you personally consider disrespectful. How frequently are you the victim of such behaviors? How frequently are you guilty of such behaviors?

4. There is considerable talk these days about how young people do not behave as well as they used to. Do you believe that this observation is correct? If so, what do you feel are some of the causes of the change?

5. Engage a group of students in a discussion of how they think acts of disrespect among students should be handled. Describe the nine approaches and have them indicate which they prefer and their reasons.

# C·H·A·P·T·E·R · E·I·G·H·T

# STUDENT DISRESPECT
# TOWARD TEACHERS

As discussed in the preceding chapter, the behaviors that constitute disrespect vary from one school to the next and from one teacher to another within the same school. A variety of student actions fall under the heading of disrespectful behavior.[1] Such diverse behaviors as verbal "put-downs," meandering around the classroom, stretching while yawning loudly, and looks of disdain all constitute disrespectful behavior at one time or another. Fred Jones, an advocate of the Classroom Management Training Program in California, claims that fully 80 percent of all classroom disruptions are incidences of disrespectful behaviors.[2] Alfred Alschuler likens schools to battlegrounds where students successfully engage in tactics to avoid paying attention to teachers more than 50 percent of the time.[3] Specific incidences of disrespectful behavior, if unchecked, tend to escalate during the school year. Walter Doyle notes how important early, apparently innocuous, rule violations are in predicting teacher control problems later in the year. Doyle's studies of student teachers illustrate that early rule violations—such as talking, note passing, and attempts at

---

1 For example, Alfred Alschuler identifies no fewer than ten categories of "basic student tactics" for avoiding doing what teachers want them to do in *School Discipline: A Socially Literate Solution* (McGraw-Hill, 1980), p. 29.

2 Fred Jones, California Workshop presentation, 1980. Jones maintains that these disrespectful behaviors are principally of two types: students talking to their neighbors in class and being out of seat in violation of the teacher's rule to be seated.

3 Alfred S. Alschuler, *School Discipline*, p. 28

4 Walter Doyle, "Classroom Management and Teacher Decision Making." Paper presented at the American Educational Research Association meeting, San Francisco, April 1979.

embarrassing the teacher—are "tests" of the teacher's classroom management ability. If the teacher fails to notice the behaviors or if the teacher's reaction indicates fear or insecurity, the frequency of these behaviors tends to increase. The number of students who violate rules also tends to increase.

Teacher and student definitions of what is and what is not disrespectful behavior may differ, of course, as we pointed out in Chapter 7. Figure 1 on page 96 suggests that some disrespectful behavior is a function of the "eyes of the beholder." Each time a behavior occurs the observer must determine whether it was accidental or intentional. The central question for this chapter is this: What can be done to reduce or eliminate disrespectful behaviors that are directed at teachers? Assertive Discipline and Logical Consequences will be highlighted.

# HANDLING STUDENT DISRESPECT TOWARD TEACHERS

Assertive Discipline and Logical Consequences entail quite different approaches to the reduction of student disrespect. Assertive Discipline places little emphasis on understanding the origins of disrespect. Instead, teachers are urged to require students to observe basic rules of politeness and to deny attention to those who fail to obey them. Logical Consequences also is concerned with rule-governed behavior, but more stress is placed on understanding the causes of disrespect. Each approach is briefly summarized below.

> I don't know what to say about Elly and her friends. Sometimes they make me so angry I could strangle them and other times they're angels to work with. The problem is that they chatter nonstop all through the class period. Yet they turn their assignments in on time and get good grades so it's hard to force them to keep quiet. But, frankly, each day gets worse. Yesterday it took me a full ten minutes to get the class quieted down so that I could begin my presentation. Next thing I knew, Elly started whispering to Sarah and that started the whole group chattering. I kept raising my voice and staring at them but they just ignored me. I kept trying to shush them up, but it finally got out of control and I had to shout to get attention. They quieted down immediately but I felt awful that I'd lost my temper.

## Assertive Discipline

| | |
|---|---|
| Key: | Rules and consequences |
| Slogan: | Say what you mean and mean what you say |
| Central Assumptions: | Teacher attitudes govern teacher behavior |
| Goal: | Allow teachers to spend as much time teaching as possible |
| Important Aspects: | Student involvement in rule making |
| | Consequences for rule breaking are public |
| | Consequences range from a warning (name on board) to detention |
| | Teacher justifies disciplinary actions to students in terms of insistence on being able to teach |
| Potential Problems: | Little provision for out-of-class behavior problems |
| | Students depend on the teacher to resolve all problems |
| | Little opportunity for collaborative conflict resolution or exploration of origins of problems |

## Logical Consequences

| | |
|---|---|
| Key: | Student responsibility |
| Goal: | Replace punishments with consequences |
| Central Assumptions: | Student behavior is goal-directed |

|  | Students learn best through concrete experiences |
| --- | --- |
| Goal: | Encourage responsible behavior |
| Important Aspects: | For individual problems, confront students with diagnosis (attention, power, revenge, display of weakness) |
|  | For classroom and school problems, involve students in rule making |
|  | Establish logical consequences for rule breaking |
|  | In resolving conflicts, teachers should not fight or give in |
| Potential Problems: | Possibility that teacher will misdiagnose an individual problem |
|  | Interventions are clinical in nature and require time |
|  | Logical consequences are difficult to develop and sometimes impossible to impose |

# *Assertive Discipline*

## Key Questions

1. *Does the problem behavior violate a classroom rule?*
2. *What is the punishment for disobeying the rule?*
3. *Have the rule and punishment been communicated to the student?*
4. *Is this rule infraction so serious that it qualifies as an immediate "severe clause"?*
5. *Do I have positive reinforcers established for students who behave appropriately?*
6. *Am I willing to assert myself and enforce the rule already established or will I ignore this behavior?*

*Does the problem behavior violate a classroom rule?* In order to deal with the problem he described, Mr. Morgan took a weekend workshop in Assertive Discipline. Prior to the workshop, he had assumed that students knew not to talk when he made class presentations. Now he realizes that he must make his classroom rules explicit. Mr. Morgan decides on the following rules, modeled after the samples given to him at the workshop:[5]

Classroom rules:
1. No talking in class without raising your hand.
2. No coming to class without pencil and materials.
3. No tardies.
4. No unexcused absences.
5. No talking loudly enough to be heard.

*What is the punishment for disobeying the rule?* One of the workshop leaders shared a typical set of punishments, designed to increase in severity for each rule violation. Mr. Morgan modified these slightly and created his own set:

| | | |
|---|---|---|
| 1st infraction | = | Student's name is written on the board. |
| 2nd infraction | = | Name plus one check mark ($\nu$) indicating that the punishment is 15 minutes' detention before or after school |
| 3rd infraction | = | Name plus two check marks — 30 minutes' detention plus a call home to the student's parents |
| 4th infraction | = | Name plus three check marks — all of the above plus a parent conference |
| 5th infraction | = | Student is immediately sent to the vice-principal (and receives all the other punishments as well). |

*Have the rule and the punishment been communicated to the student?* Mr. Morgan outlined the new rules and punishments clearly to his students and posted them prominently in his classroom. He also notified the students' families by sending home a letter describing the new program, its rationale and purposes. Morgan was careful to speak with his school administrators about the program and clarify the kind of support from them he would need.

---

5 Our thanks to Catherine Wiehe of San Jose Unified School District for sharing her application of Assertive Discipline to high school classrooms.

*Is this infraction so serious that it qualifies as an immediate "severe clause"?* Morgan realized that his set of classroom rules did not address the most serious offenses, such as physically harming another student and destroying property.

The Assertive Discipline workshop leaders pointed out that there are certain behaviors so serious that they warrant immediate removal from the classroom. In such cases, they suggested invoking the "severe clause" by sending the student immediately to the office (or asking someone to pick him up, if he refuses to leave). The student cannot then return to class until the teacher and his parents have conferenced and determined the criteria for classroom reentry.[6] Mr. Morgan did not expect to have to use this option, but he described it to his students nonetheless.

*Does the teacher have positive reinforcers established for students who behave appropriately?* After attending the workshop and reading the Assertive Discipline materials, Mr. Morgan realized that a critical element in the success of his program was a schedule of positive reinforcements for appropriate behavior. He established a number of bonuses for students who obeyed the rules — special field trips for a given number of bonus points, a box of surprise gifts (new pencils, tokens for free drinks at the student snack bar, and the like). He also established a number of group reinforcers to encourage students to help each other obey the rules. Whenever 90 percent or more of the students in a given class turned in homework assignments, he gave the class points toward a semester's end movie-and-popcorn party. Morgan varied his reinforcers to suit student interests as much as possible and to balance any negative aspects of Assertive Discipline.

*Is the teacher willing to assert himself and enforce the rules already established or will he ignore the behaviors?* In the case of Elly and her talkative friends, Mr. Morgan has to be very careful to mete out punishments fairly. Whenever a student violates a classroom rule, a name must be written on the board or a check mark noted. If the students believe that the teacher is not treating everyone equally or if he accuses innocent students of being disruptive, the system will not function effectively. Mr. Morgan must decide if he will "punish" Elly and her friends every time

---

6 Almost half of the school districts with negotiated contracts in the United States permit teachers to exclude disruptive students from class.

they talk out of turn. In some ways, the hardest choices for teachers using Assertive Discipline are those made before the classroom door opens. Teachers must decide that they alone are responsible for determining classroom rules and punishments for rule infractions. They then must select the rules most critical to effective classroom operation and those that can be enforced uniformly. Once the commitment to use Assertive Discipline has been made, the preparation completed, and the system set in place, the procedures are supposed to become automatic.

# Logical Consequences

While both Logical Consequences and Assertive Discipline share a common concern for classroom rules, they differ markedly in how students who break rules are handled. Rather than systematically applying predetermined sanctions, Logical Consequences stresses understanding the motives underlying disobedience and determining consequences that are related directly to the nature of the offense.

---

### Key Questions

1. *What is the goal of this student's inappropriate behavior?*
2. *When is a good time to talk with this student about his behavior?*
3. *What are the logical consequences of the student's behavior and how can I make the student aware of these consequences?*
4. *How can I avoid dictating a corrective procedure to the student and encourage the student to propose his own solution?*

---

*What is the goal of this student's inappropriate behavior?* Dreikurs argues that student misbehavior is the result of at least one of the following four goals: (1) attention getting, (2) power, (3) revenge, or (4) display of inadequacy. The teacher's role in classroom management is to assist the student in determining which of these (or which combination) is prompting his behavior. Corrective strategies follow from an understanding of these behavioral antecedents. In the present case, Mr. Morgan has identified Elly as the principal talker. He observes that on the days when Elly is absent there is little difficulty silencing the other students.

Identifying the reasons for Elly's talkativeness during class time is no easy matter. She is a very attractive girl and receives plenty of attention from her peers. Mr. Morgan remembers that on more than one occasion Elly has corrected the teacher's remarks about various aspects of American history (and he had to admit that Elly was correct). Why Elly should want to engage in power struggles with him was not clear, however, until he discussed this problem with a colleague. Mr. Morgan then learned that Elly's counselor forced her to repeat tenth-grade civics because her attendance had been so poor the preceding year. Elly was very upset at this turn of events and complained to her parents, both teachers in another school district. After considerable discussion, Elly's parents and counselor determined that, although she knew the subject matter, her poor attendance record warranted the repeat of tenth-grade civics. Elly was understandably distressed with her parents but, instead of solving the problem with them, she displaced her anger by giving her current civics teacher, Mr. Morgan, a difficult time.

*When is a good time to talk with this student about her behavior?* Finding time to speak with Elly during school is a problem because recent budget cutbacks have forced teachers to give up preparation periods. After school, students leave immediately to catch buses to their home areas, which often are a considerable distance from the school. Mr. Morgan decides to meet with Elly at lunchtime, even though they will have a limited time to discuss the issues.

*What are the logical consequences of Elly's behavior and how can the teacher make her aware of these consequences?* After completing an analysis of her probable motives, Mr. Morgan determines that Elly's power struggle with him is a result of her repressed anger at her parents and her desire for revenge against them. During the lunchtime conference, he outlines his analysis of her behavior. She responds initially with defensive comments but eventually agrees with Mr. Morgan's analysis. They agree to work on a plan mutually agreeable to all.

*How can the teacher avoid dictating a corrective procedure to Elly and encourage her to propose her own solution?* Mr. Morgan understands that Elly must be involved in the determination of appropriate actions to curb her inappropriate behaviors and develop more responsible ones. He suggests they work together to accelerate her academic work in civics class with the possibility that she might transfer to eleventh-grade history at the semester break. They agree in a written contract on a suitable work schedule to allow Elly to reach her goals. Mr. Morgan indicates that he will work out the details of the plan with Elly's counselor and her parents if she will agree to be responsible for her own work and behavior.

## Comparing Approaches

Assertive Discipline and Logical Consequences are perhaps best suited to individual cases of problem behavior. Assertive Discipline deals primarily with the overt behaviors exhibited by Elly and her peers rather than the origins of their behaviors. Behavior Modification is most like Assertive Discipline in this regard. Logical Consequences, on the other hand, provides a system for understanding the origins of Elly's behavior in light of the four goals identified by Rudolf Dreikurs, but leaves the working out of solutions to the teacher and students.

Transactional Analysis also presents specific procedures for dealing with disruptive behaviors. The teacher is admonished to search for the "payoff" for the student in each case of disruptive behavior by asking these questions:[7]

> Is the payoff getting applause and laughter from an audience?
> Is the payoff being bawled out or getting permission to continue being clumsy?
> Is the payoff having the teacher force the student to do something?

Once the teacher understands the payoff in TA terms, he can resist responding as the student expects and encourage more positive ways for the student to get encouragement from the teacher. As with TA and Logical Consequences, TET focuses on the nature of teacher-student communication. However, TET places more emphasis on collaborative decision making for classroom rules and insists on negotiated conflict resolution when problems arise.

PPC, Social Literacy Training, and the SMPSD provide more global approaches for dealing with disrespectful behaviors. The

---

7 Ken Ernst, *Games Students Play*, p. 38.

latter two focus primarily on schoolwide, rather than classroom-based, strategies. As a result, these approaches would not be very useful in dealing with Elly's conduct unless a number of other students were similarly disrespectful.

In the event that disrespect toward teachers is chronic, the approaches mentioned above, along with Reality Therapy, might seek to involve the student peer group in seeking and implementing solutions. Student courts, group problem solving, and peer counseling services can demonstrate that young people need not always be cast in adversarial roles. The development of responsible behavior can be facilitated by allowing students to share in the resolution of behavior problems.

## Activities

1. Question at least four of your colleagues to determine which student behaviors they consider disrespectful and what strategies they use to deal with them. What criteria does each one use to determine instances of disrespect?

2. Audiotape one of your classes, or another class if you are not teaching currently. Chart the number of times students engage in the behaviors you consider disrespectful. Next note the teacher's responses to the inappropriate behaviors. Which are not effective? Speculate on the reasons for the differences.

3. Involve your students in a lesson or unit devoted to the topic of disrespectful behavior. Have students divide into groups and act out incidents from both the teacher's and students' points of view. Discuss what you learn with the students and with other teachers.

# P·A·R·T · T·H·R·E·E

# MANAGING STUDENT BEHAVIOR YOUR WAY

To reiterate a point made in the opening of the book, current research has failed to identify any one "best" way to manage classrooms. What "works" may depend on a variety of factors, including the age and type of students involved, the experience and personality of the teacher, the subject matter, community norms, and the availability of additional resources. The concluding part of this book is intended to assist you in deciding which approach or approaches may be most useful. A set of assessment questions, incorporated into the Classroom Management Decision Guide, is provided to facilitate the process.

We would be remiss if we completed the book without mentioning some of the constraints with which you must contend. No matter how thoughtfully you select an approach and how carefully you implement it, there is no guarantee that external or unforeseen factors will not serve to inhibit or undermine your efforts. Among these are your own mental health, relations with other persons, and laws. The better you understand the potential impact on classroom management of such factors, the better prepared you will be to deal effectively with surprises.

Following the final chapter, we offer some resources for those of you who wish to learn more about classroom management. A complete set of overviews of the nine approaches discussed in this book is provided. For each approach we include specific bibliographical references and an address where further information can be obtained. A list of general references and an index also are included. We hope that these resources together with the rest of the book prove to be valuable aids as you proceed to think about classroom management. If you have suggestions or additions which might make the book more useful, please contact us.

Daniel L. Duke
Director
Educational Administration
  Program
Lewis and Clark College
Portland, Oregon 97223

Adrienne M. Meckel
c/o School of Education
Stanford University
Stanford, California 94305

# CHOOSING THE BEST
# APPROACH FOR YOU

You are or soon will be a critic and potential consumer of classroom management approaches. While selecting the approach or approaches that seem best for you may not be exactly like buying a new car, there are important similarities.

First, no approach is best for all teachers or all teaching situations. Just as different types of automobiles are appropriate for different sets of driver needs, so too must classroom management approaches be weighed in relation to a variety of factors, ranging from the age of your students to your overall goals. You do not purchase an economy compact to do the work of a four-wheel-drive all-terrain vehicle. Similarly, you would not select a classroom management approach designed for young children to use with older adolescents.

Second, *you* are in the best position to decide which approach is the most suitable one for you. No one knows your driving style, transportation needs, and available resources better than you. Likewise, no administrator, consultant, college professor, or parent knows your teaching skills or the realities of your classroom better than you. Not only do you possess more knowledge about your own teaching situation than anyone else, but you are the person who ultimately will be responsible for implementing a new classroom management approach. You also will have to live with the consequences if it fails. Therefore, it is only reasonable for you to regard yourself as the key decision maker when it comes to selecting a classroom management approach.

Even key decision makers, of course, may need help making informed decisions. If you were purchasing an automobile, you might consult friends who owned different makes, read literature from independent consumers' groups, and ask a trained mechanic to inspect prospective choices. Thus, a third similarity between choosing a car and choosing an approach to classroom management is the importance of basing your choice on as much available information concerning existing alternatives as possible.

In the preceding chapters we have tried to provide information to help you evaluate nine classroom management approaches. In this chapter we discuss what to do with that information — or how to go from reading about alternatives to committing yourself to a particular choice.

# CLASSROOM MANAGEMENT DECISION GUIDE

To assist teachers in processing large amounts of consumer information, we have created the Classroom Management Decision Guide (CMDG). This form consists of a series of questions that teachers can ask themselves *after* they are familiar with the various alternative approaches to classroom management that are available, either those described in this book or others.

The likelihood of finding the approach that is best for you is increased by considering as many approaches as possible, so it is unwise to base a decision on a consideration of only the first two or three you encounter. For this reason, we have included nine widely used and divergent approaches in our review.

The questions in the CMDG cover preliminary concerns, including your goals with regard to classroom management and your basic values, plus a variety of specific criteria, such as the age of your students, the time you have available for classroom management, and local guidelines pertaining to the treatment of students. No attempt has been made to give these selection criteria different "weights." Some will be more important than others depending on the unique concerns of each individual. The CMDG is simply a mechanism to help make the process of deciding on a classroom management approach more systematic and thorough.

Before using the CMDG, you may wish to skip ahead and read the discussion of each component of the decision guide.

# CLASSROOM MANAGEMENT
# DECISION GUIDE
## Instructions

This instrument is designed to help you decide on a classroom management approach that is best for your particular circumstances. Think about each question carefully. You may need additional sheets of paper in order to respond to the questions on the left-hand side of the page in as much detail as possible.

When you come to Section C, the questions on the right-hand side of the page are designed to force you to narrow the approaches which seem to fit the situation best. You may feel uncomfortable narrowing your responses, but you are encouraged to do so.

A. *Preliminary Questions*

What is my primary classroom management goal?

_____

_____

Which approaches to classroom management address this goal?

_____

_____

_____

What values or strongly held beliefs concerning classroom management do I have?

_____

_____

Which approaches recognize these values and beliefs?

_____

_____

_____

B. *Narrowing the Alternatives*

As a result of answering the Preliminary Questions, I feel that the following approaches to classroom management are consistent with my goals and values.

_____

_____

_____

C. *Selection Factors*

I. STUDENT CHARACTERISTICS

What is the range of maturity of my students?

_____

_____

Which of the approaches listed in Section B is best suited to this maturity range?

_____

_____

_____

What has been the past disciplinary record of my students?

_____

_____

Which of the approaches listed in Section B is best suited to this past disciplinary record?

_____

_____

_____

What are the cultural backgrounds of my students?

_____

_____

Which of the approaches listed in Section B is best suited to my students' cultural backgrounds?

_____

_____

_____

How much support can I expect from my students' parents?

_____

_____

Which of the approaches listed in Section B is best suited to the level of expected parental support?

_____

_____

_____

## II. AVAILABLE RESOURCES

How much time will I need to learn each of the classroom management approaches listed in Section B?

_____

_____

How much time do I have available for learning a new approach?

_____

_____

Which of the approaches listed in Section B is best suited to the time I have available for training?

_____

_____

_____

How much daily classroom time is likely to be needed (on average) for each approach?

_____

_____

How much time am I prepared to devote during an average day or class period to classroom management?

_____

_____

Which of the approaches listed in Section B is best suited to the time I have available for implementation?

_____

_____

_____

What special requirements of space and materials are needed to implement each approach?

_____

_____

Which of the approaches listed in Section B is best suited to the space and materials that I have available (or to which I have access)?

_____

_____

_____

What is the estimated cost in dollars of learning and implementing each approach (for a one-year period)?

_____

_____

Which of the approaches listed in Section B is least costly?

_____

_____

_____


## III. GUIDELINES

What district and school guidelines relate to classroom management?

_____

_____


What aspects of each approach might conflict with these guidelines?

_____

_____


Which of the approaches listed in Section B conflicts the least with district and school guidelines?

_____

_____

_____


D. *Choosing the Best Approach for Me*

Reviewing the information above and particularly the approaches listed in the blanks on the right-hand side of the form, select the approaches that seem to be the most promising:

_____

_____

_____

E. *Next Steps*

What must I now do in order to obtain further information on these approaches?

_____

_____

_____

To assist you in using the CMDG, we shall review each of the questions and discuss how it might be answered in light of the nine classroom management approaches covered in this book. It should be noted, though, that the CMDG also can be used to consider additional approaches, since the questions themselves are not tied to any particular approach or set of alternatives.

*What is your primary classroom management goal?* This question, along with the following one, constitute preliminary queries. The pair are so basic that all other questions are regarded as derivative. By answering these two questions, you can narrow the range of alternatives under consideration. If some of the alternatives fail to address your primary classroom management goal, you can eliminate them or else reconsider the appropriateness of your goal. In any event, only the approaches that are in accordance with your goal or goals should be considered in Section C of the CMDG.

A number of possible classroom management goals exist, and no two approaches share identical goals. Some of the more central goals of the nine approaches have been presented in Table 1 (Chapter 2). These goals included:

1. Stopping negative student behavior quickly
2. Encouraging responsible student behavior
3. Expanding conflict-resolution capacity
4. Improving teacher-student relations
5. Increasing teacher control
6. Minimizing problem-producing situations
7. Restructuring schools

It is important for teachers to realize that pursuing a goal such as stopping negative student behavior quickly may not necessarily be compatible with another goal, such as encouraging responsible student behavior. Trade-offs must be made in the selection of the classroom management approach that is best for you.

Teachers are not always clear about what they expect a classroom management approach to accomplish for them. Consider two seemingly similar goals — reducing irresponsible student behavior and increasing responsible student behavior. While they sound as if they could be addressed by the same approach, each represents a quite distinct goal and requires a different approach. In order to reduce irresponsible behavior, you may try to remove sources of temptation. Objects that can be stolen or vandalized thus would be hidden. Situations in which students are likely to misbehave — like assemblies — would be avoided.

Eliminating temptation, however, does not facilitate the acquisition of responsible behavior. If that is your goal, you need to teach students to behave responsibly and provide them with opportunities to demonstrate what they have learned. If they fail to act in a conscientious manner, then privileges should be withdrawn until such time as students feel they are prepared to behave appropriately.

Table 1 in Chapter 2 indicated the variety of goals that are addressed by particular approaches covered in this book. There are obviously other goals as well that may be important to consider. For the moment, though, let us review the seven goals in Table 1.

Interestingly, only Assertive Discipline has as a primary goal *increasing teacher control*. Other approaches may work to this end, but they are designed mainly for other purposes. The most popular goal is the *encouragement of responsible student behavior*. Presumably, if students learn to be responsible, teachers need not increase their control. Another popular goal is *stopping negative behavior quickly*, which tends to be compatible with increased teacher control. *Expanding conflict-resolution capacity* and *improving teacher-student relations* are goals that are addressed by three approaches but that are more compatible with encouraging responsible student behavior. The SMPSD, alone of all the approaches, placed prime emphasis on *reducing the situations that might give rise to problem behavior*. All the other approaches tend to focus more on people and personalities — either teacher or students — and less on situations. Three approaches aim beyond classroom management to the *restructuring of school organization*.

It is likely that you find more than one goal to be relevant. We suggest, however, that you focus on only one to begin with. Think of what you want your approach to classroom management to accomplish. Do not expect this key decision to come easily. Set aside sufficient time to consider the implications of your choice. Then, when you have put into words a single, primary goal for yourself, review what you know about the nine approaches and record the approaches that address this goal. *What values or strongly held beliefs concerning classroom management do you have?*

You may hold certain values or beliefs that are so basic to your being that everything you do is affected by them. Sometimes these values or beliefs are so ingrained that you are not even aware they exist. They seem to be an integral part of your very make-up. Before choosing the approach to classroom management that is best for you, it is important to consider these values and beliefs.

For example, you may believe that no human being has the right to strike another. Thus, no approach involving corporal punishment would be acceptable to you.

In reality, few examples are as dramatic or straightforward as corporal punishment. You typically confront choices that are ambiguous or that do not test your basic values. It is possible, however, to imagine several areas where conflict may occur.

If you believe that teachers should never relinquish control in the classroom because most students are not trustworthy, approaches that attempt to involve students in problem resolution — such as PPC, Reality Therapy, and TET — may prove unacceptable. If you believe that students should behave appropriately because they understand the importance of working together, rather than because they will be rewarded or punished, then approaches like Assertive Discipline and Behavior Modification may prove unacceptable. If you believe that the sole function of teachers is to present subject matter and evaluate student learning, then approaches that call for teachers to function as advisors and group facilitators may be inappropriate.

Think about your values and beliefs. Reflect on whether any of the classroom management approaches are in conflict with these values and beliefs. Finally, consider the reasonableness of your values and beliefs.

This last step is crucial. Far too few individuals ever seriously question their values and beliefs. To help you in this process, try a simple strategy. Write down the values and beliefs that are related to classroom management. For instance,

1. I believe that most students will try to get away with as much as they can.
2. I believe talking to students about their behavior is a waste of time.
3. I believe that the only way to stop students from misbehaving is to call their parents.

Now, treat each of your values or beliefs as a hypothesis. Be scientific. Ask yourself how you would test the hypothesis to see if it is really true. Perhaps you would decide to go back through your memory and recall your interactions with students. Even better, you might set aside the next month for collecting data to prove or disprove your "hypotheses."

Once you have reflected on your values and beliefs and tested them, you may wish to reconsider their validity. In any event, your likelihood of making a sensible choice of a classroom management approach will be increased by thinking carefully about what you believe.

## Narrowing the Alternatives

Having addressed the preliminary questions, you are now in a position to rule out approaches that do not serve your classroom management goal or that conflict with your values and beliefs. Once the list of approaches has been narrowed, it is time to ask specific questions. These questions require you to consider various sources of information about your students, your school, and yourself and to come up with your "best judgment" about each. In other words, the questions in the remainder of the CMDG do not call for precisely quantified responses. Following each question, you will be asked to review the classroom management approaches that have not been eliminated and to choose one or more that best suits your situation. This "forced choice" exercise is designed to start you thinking about making an actual commitment to adopt an approach or two. We do not believe, though, that only one approach will work for you. In many cases, you may borrow elements from various approaches and construct your own unique hybrid.

*What is the range of maturity of your students?* Anyone who has worked very long with students knows that some techniques are more effective with certain students than others. Students differ in countless ways, but certain differences seem to be particularly crucial when choosing a classroom management approach. The maturity level of students is one such factor.

Maturity level refers to a student's stage of growth — in particular, psychological growth. The best predictor of maturity is age, but it is not foolproof. Sometimes young children are capable of assuming adultlike responsibilities; in other cases adolescents may be unable to transcend childlike concerns.

Researchers have studied various dimensions of maturity, from moral development to cognitive growth. For us the key elements of maturity relate to a student's ability to understand the purpose of school and classroom rules, to comprehend the role of the teacher, and to assume responsibility for his own behavior. Less mature students often fail to grasp the value of rules in group settings, to appreciate the complexity of the teacher's task, and to realize that they harm themselves by failing to cooperate.

Some of the approaches to classroom management are better suited to mature students than others. For example, approaches emphasizing group process — like PPC and TET — call on students to exhibit considerable maturity. While these approaches also are useful vehicles for teaching students to behave responsibly, they are probably inappropriate for very immature students, particularly those who lack verbal skills.

The abstract reasoning ability of students also is a component of maturity that may bear on your choice of an approach. For example, Logical Consequences and TA require students to be confronted with and to understand the motives underlying their behavior. Abstract reasoning ability often is not present in less mature students.

Less mature students are likely to respond more quickly to approaches that involve immediate reinforcement or punishment. Assertive Discipline and Behavior Modification are two such approaches. As students mature, teachers have greater difficulty locating reinforcers or punishments that "matter." Appeals to reason seem to be more practical with mature students.

Many teachers work with heterogeneous groups of students. Maturity levels in one class can range from childlike to adult. You probably will need to base part of your choice of an approach on your best estimate of the maturity level of the majority of your students. Where you have substantial minorities of either less or more mature students, special provisions such as a more individualized type of discipline may be justified.

*What has been the past disciplinary record of your students?* Probably the single best predictor of how a student will behave in your class is how he has behaved in previous classes. Information on past disciplinary experiences is usually available from other teachers, administrators, guidance personnel, parents, and the students themselves. As in the case of maturity, it is likely that your students will encompass a wide range of past disciplinary experiences. Some may have been labeled behavior disordered, some may have been chronic truants, and others — probably most — will have had few if any disciplinary difficulties.

One of the approaches — PPC — originally was designed expressly for groups of young people in which *everyone* had experienced prior behavior problems. Several other approaches are oriented to settings characterized by relatively large numbers of students with records of behavior problems. These include Assertive Discipline, Behavior Modification, and SMPSD. Reality Therapy, along with PPC, can be useful when one or two students have histories of behavior problems and you feel there is value in engaging the entire class in an effort to resolve present difficulties.

*What are the cultural backgrounds of your students?* One of the greatest challenges facing teachers today is how to deal effectively with students from different cultures in the same classroom. Much has been written about the difficulties white teachers encounter trying to understand the culture-based behavior of blacks, Chicanos, and other racial and ethnic minorities. These teachers often regard different styles of dress, speech, and mannerisms as disrespectful, when, in fact, they merely are part of the culture in which certain students have been raised. Punishing a black student for wearing a stocking cap in class or avoiding looking you squarely in the eye when you are addressing him may be unfair if the student has grown up taking such behavior for granted.

Some of the approaches seem to possess greater flexibility for accommodating different culture-based behaviors than others. An approach such as Assertive Discipline that focuses on a single set of rules and that does not differentiate between causes of rule breaking probably may be less suited to classes with students from different cultures than approaches like TET or Social Literacy Training, which involve student and teacher in sharing perceptions of the "problem." None of the approaches, however, actually can substitute for learning about the mores of minority cultures. We believe that most teachers can benefit greatly from such instruction.

*How much support can you expect from your students' parents?*
Some approaches rely more on parental support than others, so it
will be important for you to assess the extent to which your students' parents are willing to be involved in dealing with classroom
behavior problems. Approaches that emphasize rules and punishments for disobedience tend to count on parental involvement as
a "last resort" when sanctions fail. Approaches that try to encourage students to behave responsibly frequently avoid parental involvement entirely. The expectation is that students who create
problems will participate in resolving them. The SMPSD is one of
the few approaches that seeks to encourage the growth of student
responsibility without overlooking the value of parental involvement. In order for the SMPSD to be fully implemented, parents
and students both are expected to help develop school rules and
sanctions and to participate in conflict-resolution activities.

It may be hard for you to estimate how much parental support
to expect. We believe that most parents *want* to help out when their
own children are involved. Fewer parents may desire to provide
general assistance, say in rule making. Unfortunately, parents
often lack the time to become involved in classroom management. The increase in single-parent families and families where
both parents work has contributed to the problem. In addition,
minority parents often are suspicious of educators and fearful that
any direct intervention on their part will lead to embarrassment
for them or reprisals against their children.

*How much time will you need to learn each of the classroom
management approaches described in Part II?* The preceding set
of questions concerned student characteristics. The immediate
question and those that follow relate to available resources, particularly time, space, materials, and money. The feasibility of
successfully implementing a particular approach is tied closely to
the availability of these resources.

Time is the scarcest commodity in any teacher's life. Teaching
is simply one of those jobs for which there are always more things
to do than time available. In selecting an approach to classroom
management, you need to consider how much time it will take to
learn the approach and how much time you are willing to devote
to the task.

Some approaches require more training than others.[1] TET, for
example, is taught in a thirty-hour workshop. The basic prin-

---

[1] Information on training in various approaches is constantly changing. We advise
readers to contact training programs directly, using addresses provided in the Reference section.

ciples of a particular Behavior Modification technique may be learned in an evening's reading. You already possess some skills and knowledge related to each approach by virtue of having read this book, so you will not be starting from scratch. It is important to determine what you already know and how much time in addition to the initial workshop or training course will be required before mastery of an approach can reasonably be expected. If you are unable to attend a workshop or training course, you may decide to explore some of the approaches through books and articles, but this mode of learning does not permit you either to see the approaches in action or to practice them in controlled settings. In addition, most approaches are constantly evolving or being modified, making books and articles somewhat outdated. It is generally advisable to budget time to visit other teachers who already are using particular approaches and observe them in action. Many schools provide released time for teachers to undertake such professional development activities.

*How much daily classroom time is likely to be needed for each approach?* The time it takes to learn an approach is one concern. The time required to implement and maintain it is quite another. The approaches that are based on teacher-student conferences and group discussions may entail a relatively large investment of time. None of the approaches actually specifies how much classroom time may be needed, but you should try estimating how long regular conferences or discussions are likely to take. The sessions prescribed in PPC probably require the largest regular investment of time, with Reality Therapy and TET close behind. The SMPSD and Social Literacy Training call for group work at intervals, either during the first few weeks of each school year or as problems arise. Thus, the investment of time is not constant for these approaches. Logical Consequences and TA call for private conferences with students. Time for these conferences may be available during class, assuming provisions can be made to keep other students busy. Otherwise you must expect to utilize time before, between, or after classes. Assertive Discipline and Behavior Modification probably entail the least amount of implementation time once the initial development of rules or establishment of reinforcement schedules is accomplished.

All of the approaches will require you periodically to take time outside class to assess how well they are working. The SMPSD also calls for teachers to meet together on a regular basis to try and anticipate problems before they get out of hand. Only you know how much out-of-class time you are likely to need to implement an approach, but we advise you to expect occasionally to spend time planning, evaluating, and conferring with colleagues. Without this kind of reflective activity, even the best of approaches can develop problems.

Once you estimate how much in-class and out-of-class time the approaches will take to implement and maintain, you must decide how much time you are prepared to devote to classroom management. In order to make this decision you probably will need to review the preceding questions concerning student characteristics to get an idea of the types of students with whom you'll be working. It is important to remember that the approach which entails the least investment of time may not always be the best one for you and your particular group of students. There are other worthwhile goals besides efficiency.

*What special requirements of space and materials are needed to implement each approach?* As a teacher you must spend some of your energy allocating scarce resources. Time is one of the scarcest of these resources. Space and materials also tend to be available in limited supply.

The only space requirements of the approaches are suitable places to hold group discussions and private conferences. Group discussions can be accommodated comfortably in any room with movable furniture. If your room is unsuitable, you may have access to some relatively quiet space in a vacant room or unused part of the campus. It is important, however, that meeting areas are located within reasonable walking distance of class, since the effectiveness of group discussions often depends on timing. A long walk to reach a meeting area or other logistical problems can cause a loss of enthusiasm or even contribute to additional behavior problems.

Adequate space for individual conferences with students during class time typically is unavailable to teachers because most classrooms are not equipped with private alcoves which still permit teachers to see what the class is doing. Meeting in the hallway may be acceptable under some circumstances, but often privacy is lacking and classroom supervision impossible. If no one is available to supervise your students while you conduct a conference away from class, you may be forced to schedule it for a time when your room or some other facility is unoccupied.

Special materials are not required by most of the approaches described in this book. Behavior Modification techniques, however, sometimes call for equipment such as counters, watches, and buzzers. In addition, concrete reinforcers, like candy or pencils, often are used, particularly with younger students. As students grow older, privileges, free time, and other "intangibles" tend to replace these objects. Social Literacy Training involves several games that may require some paraphernalia. The SMPSD calls for the collection of data on student behavior problems, a process that necessitates various forms and files. Other than these examples, the approaches do not require equipment or materials.

*What is the estimated cost in dollars of learning and implementing each approach?* Training in each of the approaches is available in workshops offered by consultants and, in some cases, in college and in-service courses. When the training is required by your employer, the cost is typically assumed by the school district. Otherwise you may have to pay out of your own pocket. If you are already employed as a teacher and you enroll in a course or workshop that is intended for professional improvement rather than the acquisition of a credential or degree, you are permitted to claim the cost of training as a tax deduction, however.

The prices of workshops vary according to location (travel expenses often must be absorbed by workshop participants), reputation of the presenter (originators are more expensive than disciples), and size of group (larger groups generally involve lower costs per participant). Prices also vary over time. When this book was written, for example, the cost per participant for a fourteen-hour training course in the SMPSD was $20. Assertive Discipline averaged $25 a person for a one-day workshop. Factors such as demand and inflation contribute to fluctuations in prices. You therefore are advised to contact consultants directly for a price quotation.

In some instances it may be possible for you to reduce the cost of training by pooling resources with several colleagues. One person may receive training on the condition that he shares his knowledge with his cohorts afterwards. In other cases, you may be able to train yourself by obtaining literature on an approach and forming a reading group with colleagues. Books are available on all nine approaches, though Assertive Discipline materials can be obtained only by workshop participants.

*What district and school guidelines relate to classroom management?* As student behavior problems have increased during the last decade, more schools and districts have developed detailed codes of conduct for students and disciplinary guidelines for teachers. This trend also derives impetus from the student rights movement and greater involvement of courts in cases involving student behavior. Schools are expected to specify what behavior is expected of students, guarantee that these expectations do not violate the rights of students, and ensure that the punishments for acting inappropriately are administered fairly. While it is difficult to estimate the extent to which most teachers actually are aware of or comply with disciplinary guidelines, you are advised to take them into consideration before selecting a classroom management approach.

It is conceivable, for example, that a particular approach conflicts with a local guideline. A school that requires certain student behavior problems to be referred to the office may not be a good place to implement approaches calling for classroom discussion and resolution of all student problems. Of course, guidelines can be changed. If you feel strongly that a particular approach is best for you, you are encouraged to explore the possibility of having restrictive guidelines modified or eliminated. Teachers typically are in a better position than school officials to know which policies are and are not constructive.

## Choosing the Best Approach for You

After you have reflected on and answered all the questions in the first three sections of the CMDG, you are prepared to identify the approaches that seem best for you. Obviously, you have not considered everything, but you have touched on most of the salient factors.

No decision is so carefully made that it will not require periodic reevaluation. Classroom, school, and personal circumstances change. As they do, you may need to review the CMDG. In addition, you may hear about new approaches to classroom management. While it is crucial to be committed to the approach or approaches you are implementing at any given time, it is also important to avoid blind devotion and keep in touch with new alternatives. Scheduling periodic reevaluations of your decision reduces the likelihood that you will become too attached to particular approaches.

Reevaluating your decision also permits you to ascertain the extent to which you actually have implemented the approach or approaches you intended to implement. A particular approach may fail because it has been implemented incorrectly, not because it is a poor approach. If you never look systematically at how you are using a set of strategies and techniques and the impact it is having, you will probably be unable to determine whether to abandon all of them or simply modify a few.

Some questions you may wish to ask in conducting an assessment of your choice of classroom management approaches include the following:

1. What goal or goals do I expect classroom management to achieve?
2. To what degree do my goals have to be achieved for me to be satisfied?
3. Over what period of time do I have to collect data to be convinced that the goal or goals are being achieved?
4. What types of data (office referrals, reprimands, intentions, minutes of on-task behavior, grades, completed assignments, etc.) can I use to determine the degree to which my goals have been achieved?
5. Using these data, what is the discrepancy between what I intended to achieve and what I actually achieved?
6. Did I implement my approach(es) according to the guidelines prescribed by the author(s)?
7. Would any other approach be more likely to achieve similar results at less cost (in terms of time, energy, resources)?
8. Would any other approach be more likely to achieve greater results?

One final point needs to be emphasized. Making decisions is a stressful process. Often it is easier simply to react to classroom situations as they arise, without going through the steps of learning about different approaches to classroom management and selecting one to implement. We believe, however, that expecting the choice-making process to be stressful can offset some of this uneasiness. We also believe that acting in accordance with a carefully thought out and investigated decision is generally preferable to merely reacting to problems as they arise.

## *Final Considerations*

We have achieved the primary purpose of this book—an analysis of nine popular approaches to classroom management and the introduction of a strategy for selecting the approaches that are best for you. We would be negligent, however, if we concluded without a discussion of some of the factors besides your choice of an approach which may influence your effectiveness as a classroom manager. The closing chapter looks at teacher mental health, problems related to the role of classroom manager, and the legal dimensions of classroom management.

# COPING WITH CONSTRAINTS

The preceding chapters describe nine approaches to managing student behavior problems and a strategy for selecting a suitable management approach. These chapters focus on three of the assumptions with which we opened this book:

1. Classroom management is an integral part of teaching.
2. Teachers can be trained to handle behavior problems effectively.
3. Teachers are in the best position to determine how they most effectively can manage their classrooms.

Having the skills and knowledge to be an effective classroom manager, however, still does not ensure that you will be able to fully demonstrate your talents or that your teaching will be problem-free. In fact, it is assumption number 4 — "Teachers often are so busy reacting to day-to-day problems that they fail to reflect on the purposes of classroom management" — which so concerned us that we were motivated to write this book and to include this final chapter. We believe that successful classroom managers are reflective, thorough in their planning, and therefore creative, rather than reactive, in their dealings with students. However, classroom management effectiveness may be inhibited by factors to which we have only briefly alluded in other chapters. Teacher mental health, staff and student relationships, and legal decisions can be constraints on teacher effectiveness. Thus this chapter provides a description of each potential constraint, suggestions and alternative actions for coping with constraints, and a set of three case studies derived from actual teacher problems in these areas.

While you may not currently be affected by all of these constraints, being aware of them can help you minimize their negative impact if and when need be.

## Teacher Mental Health

All of you face concerns in your private lives that affect your public work lives. Teachers are affected by illnesses, family problems, financial worries, and other hazards of contemporary life. Teachers also must deal with the emotional stresses and strains of a service-oriented profession in which the lives of children are entrusted to their care. We read a lot about how much teachers influence students, but insufficient attention is given to the ways in which students influence teachers. Every teacher, to varying degrees, serves as counselor, confessor, and surrogate parent to students during the school year. Helping students with their personal problems is an important part of successful student-teacher relationships, but such work can sap the energy of a conscientious teacher.

While often exhausting, ministering to the personal needs of students is potentially one of the most satisfying aspects of teaching. Teaching, after all, has a long tradition of service orientation and those who have been attracted to the profession often have had as their primary goals such altruistic purposes as "inspiring students to value learning."[1] In a profession whose members have never been highly paid, extrinsic rewards—money, prestige, power—have been less valued than psychic rewards.

Because teachers typically work alone, however, psychic rewards nearly always come from students, not from colleagues. Most teachers are physically isolated from one another in their classrooms and see supervisory personnel infrequently during the school year. Teachers rarely see a colleague teach or have any opportunities to get feedback on their own work—except from students. Small wonder, then, that how students behave and how they do their work become the indicators teachers use to evaluate their daily performance. The success or failure of instruction on a daily basis affects teacher self-esteem.

Self-esteem serves as a barometer of emotional and physical health. How well teachers think they are doing affects how they

---

[1] Dan C. Lortie, *Schoolteacher* (Chicago: The University of Chicago Press, 1975), p. 105.

feel about themselves. Nagging problems with even a single student can cloud a teacher's perception of how well things are going in general. That student behavior is an important source of teacher anxiety has been documented by stress researchers. One review of research revealed the sources of strain to be different for beginning and experienced teachers.[2] Beginning teachers reported anxiety derived from

> (a) students' liking of them; (b) their inability to maintain classroom discipline; (c) knowledge of subject matter; (d) what to do in case they make mistakes or run out of material; (e) how to relate personally to other faculty members, the school system, and parents.

Experienced teachers reported that their chief sources of anxiety related to

> (a) time demands; (b) difficulties with pupils; (c) large class enrollments; (d) financial constraints; and (e) lack of educational resources.

Classroom management matters, though, were anxiety provoking for both beginning and experienced teachers.

This is hardly surprising news. Anyone who has taught needs little reminding that student behavior problems are stressful. What teacher has not been overwhelmed by frustration or angered to the point of losing control by the actions of students. That these are not uncommon concerns, however, makes it more distressing that there are not systematic means for coping with these concerns.

Teacher mental health can be influenced by organizational realities as well as student behavior. Large class enrollments, official paperwork, and lack of educational resources are but a few of the problems teachers face from time to time. In one study of an urban high school, we chronicled the effects of budget and resource cutbacks on teachers and students.[3] The report was distressing. Teachers found that they had more to do (larger class sizes) with less time and fewer resources. They felt trapped in a downward spiral characterized by increased workload leading to increased job dissatisfaction and then to declining effectiveness.

---

2 Thomas Coates and Carl Thoresen, "Teacher Anxiety: A Review with Recommendations," *Review of Educational Research*, Vol. 46, no. 3 (Spring 1976), pp. 164–165.

3 Daniel L. Duke and Adrienne M. Meckel, "The Slow Death of a Public High School," *Phi Delta Kappan*, Vol. 61, no. 10 ( June 1980): 674–677.

As effectiveness dropped, student attendance worsened and more able students transferred to other schools. The proportion of lower-ability students continued to grow, leading to greater teacher frustration and burnout.

In some ways, teachers' expectations of themselves influenced their mental health as much as the organizational realities. Teachers knew what they had been able to do in past years with their students. The worsening conditions meant that teachers would have to lower their expectations for what could be done and that prospect was demoralizing indeed.

## Staff and Student Relationships

Several of the management approaches discussed in this book — specifically, Positive Peer Culture, Social Literacy, and the SMPSD — require cooperative efforts to produce change. Teachers must work with one another, students, parents, and school principals to structure conditions conducive to collaborative problem solving. The willingness of the various role-group members to participate in such activities influences individual teacher effectiveness.

Unfortunately, teachers are often isolated from colleagues and have little time at school to exchange ideas or problem-solving strategies. Parents and students also may be interested in discussion of classroom management problems but are reluctant to participate because they feel inexperienced in school policy making or intimidated by school administrators.

The nature of the principal's style of leadership also influences teacher effectiveness. All of the management approaches require some degree of support from school administrators. For example, Assertive Discipline requires that the principal commit time and energy to dealing with any students who have been sent out of class when the teacher invokes the "severe clause." If the principal is reluctant to assist the teacher, the teacher's ability to implement a successful Assertive Discipline program is diminished.

The norms for teacher-student relationships must also be taken into account when estimating how successful a classroom management program will be. Some school environments are "open" and encourage dialogues on school issues between teachers and students; others emphasize separation of teachers and discourage collaborative projects. In the latter case, approaches such as the

SMPSD and Social Literacy might be poorly received. Teachers who understand local conditions will not be unduly distressed by initial resistance. Prepared teachers can modify their expectations for program implementation based on their knowledge of local receptivity to the various classroom management styles.

# Legal Constraints

Outside the domain of the individual teacher but exercising an ever-increasing influence on local classroom management policies and practices are legal precedents. These have appeared as a result of state and federal court decisions over the past two decades. An exhaustive analysis of these potential constraints is not yet possible because the area is so rapidly changing. However, in two areas—suspension from school and/or class and setting school/classroom rules—enough rulings have been made so that guidelines can be discussed.

## Suspension

Since the late 1960s and landmark cases such as *Tinker* v. *Des Moines* and *Wood* v. *Strickland*, the courts have indicated that they will act in matters concerning student rights and responsibilities. Suspension from school became an issue because it was evident that minority students were disproportionally represented among suspended students. Criticizing school suspension policies for denying students "equal educational opportunity," the courts have ruled that students must be given all rights of due process— including a written statement of allegation, a hearing, and opportunity to be fairly represented—when they are suspended from school.[4]

Suspension from class has not yet been challenged in the courts, so in states such as California (which gives teachers the power to exclude students from class for a given period of time), teachers are not required to give students due process rights when ordering them to leave class. If suspension from class becomes a legal issue, management approaches such as Assertive Discipline, which advises teachers to exclude students from class or activities as deemed necessary, may be forced to modify their strategies.

---

[4] Edmund Reutter, *The Courts and Student Conduct* (Topeka, Kan.: The National Organization on Legal Problems of Education, 1975), p. 7.

In the meantime, teachers may find that principals already are reluctant to support management approaches that encourage suspension from class. Principals fear that students suspended from class will leave campus rather than go to the principal's office. Administrators know that when students are off campus, they are susceptible to injury. School personnel also may be potentially liable for damage suits.

## Classroom Rules

A number of the classroom management programs assume that teachers or teachers and students together determine the rules for student behavior in the classroom. While the courts have recognized that teachers and administrators need the authority to set rules regulating student conduct (provided these do not conflict with school board policies or higher legal mandates), the courts again have shown a primary concern for the due process rights of students. To assist in the development of school and classroom rules, Edmund Reutter studied hundreds of federal and state court decisions and distilled the following guidelines:[5]

1. The rule must be publicized to students. Whether it is issued orally or in writing, school authorities must take reasonable steps to bring the rule to the attention of students.
2. The rule must have a legitimate educational purpose.
3. The rule must have a rational relationship to the achievement of the stated educational purpose.
4. The meaning of the rule must be reasonably clear. The rule must not be so vague that it is almost completely subject to the interpretation of the school authority invoking it.
5. The rule must be sufficiently narrow in scope so as not to encompass constitutionally protected activities along with those which constitutionally may be proscribed in the school setting.
6. If the rule infringes a fundamental constitutional right of students, a compelling interest of the school (state) in the enforcement of the rule must be shown.

Reutter's guidelines are straightforward, so much so that busy teachers and administrators might tend to overlook them. Unfortunately, legal rulings cannot be ignored. School personnel must be informed of the potential legal liabilities attached to their actions and be prepared to defend their decisions. We live in a time when students who feel their rights have been violated and their

---

[5] Edmund Reutter, *The Courts and Student Conduct*, p. 6.

parents are more likely to take their concerns to legal counsel. While teachers should not be intimidated by the prospect that legal action may be taken against them, it is wise to prepare for the possibility.

## *Coping with Constraints: Suggestions and Alternative Actions*

Coping successfully with the factors discussed in this chapter requires that teachers be active information seekers utilizing various means to meet constraints head-on. Additional characteristics of effective coping behavior have been identified by Gerald Caplan:[6]

1. Active exploration of reality issues and search for information.
2. Free expression of both positive and negative feelings and a tolerance of frustration.
3. Active invoking of help from others.
4. Breaking down problems into manageable bits and working them through one at a time.
5. Awareness of fatigue and tendencies toward disorganization with pacing of efforts and maintenance of control in as many areas of functioning as possible.
6. Active mastery of feelings where possible and acceptance of inevitability where not. Flexibility and willingness to change.
7. Basic trust in oneself and others and basic optimism about outcome.

Successful coping entails understanding the demands of situations requiring personal adjustment, knowing which resources are available to aid the individual in dealing with problem situations, and possessing a self-awareness that enables the individual to know when personal resources are being overly taxed. Effective classroom managers must understand when their threshold of frustration with a particular student or group of students has been reached. They must then know to whom to turn for additional aid — which staff members can be of assistance, which colleagues have had similar problems and handled them successfully, and which community persons or agencies are valuable referrals.

---

6 Gerald Caplan's characteristics are quoted in Rudolf H. Moos, ed., *Human Adaptation: Coping with Life Crises* (Lexington, Mass.: D. C. Heath & Co., 1976), p. 14.

TABLE 4 • TEACHER MENTAL HEALTH: AFFECTED BY STUDENT BEHAVIOR

| Individual Action | Group Action |
|---|---|
| • obtain private counseling to better understand your emotional reactions to student behavior problems | • organize in-service programs at the local school, district level or at teacher centers to provide systematic training in dealing with emotions (such as counselors and social workers receive) |
| • meet privately with other teachers weekly or bi-monthly after school hours to share concerns and successful strategies for maintaining physical and mental health | • organize regular rap sessions with student groups to better understand student concerns and encourage teacher-student discussions of each group's mental health needs |

Example of a teacher stress-reduction program: The Teacher Enthusiasm Renewal course taught in Butler, Lawrence, and Mercer counties (Pennsylvania) focuses on improvement of teacher self-image and morale. Course originator Ken Musko includes trust building, problem solving, and challenging physical activities (jumping off roofs on ropes, running obstacle courses) in a four-session course for teachers.

## TEACHER MENTAL HEALTH: AFFECTED BY ORGANIZATIONAL REALITIES

| Individual Action | Group Action |
|---|---|
| • transfer to another school where the environment is less demoralizing | • lobby for redistribution of district resources to schools with greatest needs |
| • reevaluate expectations for what students "ought" to accomplish each year | • organize community resource committees to aid in raising additional funds for beleaguered schools from local businesses and industry |
| • involve higher-ability students in teaching lower-ability students (as tutors, small-group leaders) | • arrange for schoolwide tutorial programs (with peers, local college students, and parents serving as tutors) to aid lower-ability student |

Example of school reorganization: The Tucson Community Education Program in Arizona has reconceptualized the elementary school as the center of community education activities. Besides providing a variety of educational programs, the project assists teachers with classroom management by involving parents and community volunteers as attendance monitors and counselors, freeing teachers for individual and small-group conferences. In this way, it has been possible to prevent minor concerns from escalating into discipline problems.

## TABLE 5 • STAFF AND STUDENT RELATIONSHIPS

| Individual Action | Group Action |
|---|---|
| • identify the strengths of colleagues in dealing with classroom management problems | • ask for time at faculty meetings to discuss student behavior concerns and personal philosophies of management |
| • determine which administrators will provide support when needed | • ask the principal to spend more time visiting classrooms (and perhaps teach a class occasionally) so that he or she becomes more aware of teacher concerns |
| • visit individual parents on a regular basis to learn about their parenting styles and management philosophies and beliefs | |
| • team with other teachers or parent volunteers to create time to conference with individual students and determine how to improve teacher-student relationships | • discuss ways to make parents more at ease on campus and involved in school activities (publish parent newsletters, involve parents in school-rule creation, organize workshops to aid parents in dealing with problem children) |

Example of management program for parents:  After hearing teachers frequently complain that parents did not support school management policies, a junior high school counselor began an evening rap session with interested parents. Publicized simply as a time for parents to get together, discuss their concerns about raising their children, and share what worked for them, the rap sessions quickly became so popular that groups began meeting three nights a week at the school. The counselor discovered that parents did want help with their children but were intimidated by school personnel. Once the evening sessions became a regular feature of the school program, he invited teachers and parents to listen to each other's concerns about student behavior. Teachers and parents praised the evening discussion groups and supported them for several years. Unfortunately, the program was discontinued when the counselor transferred to another area.

## TABLE 6 • LEGAL CONSTRAINTS

| Individual Action | Group Action |
|---|---|
| • keep informed of current legal issues by reading law articles in education journals, state law digests and summaries | • ask a union representative to arrange for regular "briefings" for teachers on legal issues by experts |
| • document carefully all serious student behavior problems; keep an anecdotal log or file of all referral forms | • lobby for legal protection necessary for teachers in dealing with classroom management problems |

As one way of presenting the many alternatives for coping with constraints on teacher classroom management effectiveness, we have collected in the preceding tables examples of actions that can be initiated by individuals and groups of teachers. While these have been successful at selected schools, they are not appropriate for all teachers and all settings and must be evaluated in light of the context in which you work.

## ANALYSIS OF SPECIFIC CASE STUDIES

Reading about suggestions for coping with potential constraints on classroom management effectiveness and studying tables of alternatives is not enough. One way to develop and refine coping skills is to analyze sample cases illustrating real teacher problems and record or role-play reactions. In this section we provide three hypothetical cases derived from the material discussed in this chapter. If you are reading this book for a course, your instructor may ask you to divide into groups, work on these for several days, and then report to the entire class. If you are reading this book on your own, we suggest that you skim the three cases, select one of particular interest, and work on that case according to the instructions presented. In this way, you will derive maximum benefit from the exercise. Each case study begins with an interview in which an individual describes a problem. Instructions for dealing with the specifics of the problem follow each excerpt.

## *Case Study 1*

Teacher interview: "I've been a classroom teacher for seven years and have worked at this school all that time. I've seen things get steadily worse over the years to the point where I'm just fed up. Yesterday I gave my request for transfer to the principal. I've got to get out of here. The kids aren't the same because I'm not the same. I just don't have enough time with them to do what I want to do. My classes are bulging at the seams. I've got thirty-five kids in classrooms set up for twenty-four. How do they expect me to work with all those kids? I can't even find enough chairs for everybody. I know it's all getting to me because I can't sleep at night and I keep getting headaches in the afternoon. A couple of drinks at the corner bar relaxes me after school but I don't want to get in the habit. You know what really bothers me? I'm a good teacher . . . well, I was a good teacher until all these cutbacks wiped out my materials and jammed my classes. I knew what I was doing but they kept changing the rules on me . . . maybe I shouldn't be in teaching anymore.

## Instructions

You are a colleague of the teacher interviewed in Case Study 1. You believe that he is an excellent teacher and that his transfer would be a serious loss to your school staff. You want to help him cope with his frustrations.

1. Prepare a description of a helping plan for the teacher.
2. Include in your plan suggestions for utilizing the following resources:
   a. colleagues
   b. administrators, district personnel
   c. community resources (counselors, teacher centers, etc.)
3. After you have completed your written work, role-play this case and your suggestions with a colleague. Obtain written and oral feedback on the usefulness of your suggestions. Revise your helping plan as needed on the basis of the feedback you receive.

# Case Study 2

Parent interview: "Look, you teachers are all alike. You're out to get my son Joey. He hasn't got a chance here—you never give him a break. He's a good boy at home. He causes problems every once in a while . . . what kid doesn't? But he's no troublemaker like you say he is. What do you think you're doing by kicking him out of school—why should he get suspended? How's he going to learn anything if you keep kicking him out of school? And, look, I don't like the way you call me at work to pick Joey up and take him home. It's not fair to me and, besides, it gets embarrassing. My kid's just as good as anybody else's. Stop hassling him and give him a chance."

## Instructions

You are the teacher responsible for initiating the action to suspend Joey from school. This interview excerpt is taken from the conference you attended with Joey, his mother, and the school principal. The principal has said little in the conference and seems to be waiting for you to reply to Joey's mother.

1. Prepare a statement in which you respond to the parent's allegations.

2. Include the answers to these questions in your statement:
   a. Why have you asked that Joey be suspended? What educational purpose might such an action serve?
   b. What evidence do you have for incidents of Joey's misbehavior? What about his academic work?
   c. Has the school followed the necessary procedures outlined by the law for suspension from school? How?
3. Role-play this case asking classmates or colleagues to alternate taking the roles of parent, Joey, principal, and teacher. After the exercise, evaluate your actions and brainstorm additional ways of aiding Joey, calming his mother, and gaining effective support from the apparently uncommitted principal.

# Case Study 3

Teacher interview:[7] "I was so angry I could hardly see straight. I didn't even know what I was doing. When I turned around that corner and saw that bully beating up poor little Jamie, my blood boiled! I raced up to them and grabbed Randy by the arm and shook him as hard as I could. I think he was as shocked as I was by my actions . . . but I was so angry at him for picking on a smaller kid like that. As I was shaking him, I suddenly realized what I was doing—how I'd lost control of my temper and all—and I felt queasy in the knees. I just got sort of weak all over and I let go of Randy. I don't know what really happened next. Randy just seemed to fall down on the ground in a funny twisted-up way. I still don't understand how he could have broken his arm, but maybe I dropped him harder than I thought. I just don't know. The next day, the principal called me into the office to tell me that the parents were going to file suit against me. I couldn't believe it."

## Instructions

Interview five classroom teachers at both elementary and secondary levels. Include in your interview schedule the following kinds of questions:

1. Have you ever been moved to anger by a student's behavior? What did you do to deal with your emotions?

---

[7] Dramatization of this case is hypothetical, but a similar case is recorded in *Frank v. Orleans Parish School Board*, 195 So. 2d 451 (La. 1967). In that case, the court determined that the teacher's efforts in restraining the student were excessive and awarded the student $2,500 in damages.

2. What would you do to solve the problem in this case?
3. Could a colleague have helped you in this case? How?
4. Would you have used an on-campus counseling service if such were available to staff members? Why or why not?
5. In this case, what other actions were open to the teacher? What resources might have been of use?
6. What on-campus resources, support groups, community referrals would you suggest to help teachers with their mental health? What is available in your school or local community?

After analyzing your interview data, prepare a statement describing a helping plan to assist the teacher in Case Study 3. Ask your classmates (or the teachers you interviewed) to evaluate your helping plan.

In each of the cases, awareness of the issues is not sufficient for solving the problems. Emotions must be dealt with, additional resources must be located, evidence must be collected — preferably in advance of the crisis. None of these cases reflects an incident in which the teacher could solve the problem alone. Parents, legal agents, and other staff members are involved — sometimes making problems more difficult by their presence, sometimes contributing to problem resolution. Teaching may occur in isolation from other adults, but problems often escape the confines of a single classroom.

# Teacher Leadership In and Out of the Classroom

Our conception of the teacher as both an effective classroom manager and a concerned colleague requires individuals to devote time to planning and anticipating problems. In order to foster creative, rather than reactive, decision making, we have maintained that teachers must continuously seek information, skills, and resources while being reflective about what they do and why. We believe that teachers who do so become successful managers and indeed are in the best position to determine how they most effectively can manage their classrooms.

These teachers are leaders. It is from the ranks of such teacher leaders that constructive solutions to classroom management problems emerge. The constraints we have enumerated must be dealt with from the inside — both professionally and personally. Teachers must ask that these concerns be brought to the bargaining tables and then negotiate to reduce teacher liability where possible; teachers must develop effective support groups for each other and assist other role groups—parents and students—in doing the same. Perhaps most important, it is teachers who must acknowledge the final assumption of this book: Teaching is one of the most important, challenging and frustrating occupations in contemporary society.

Believing in one's teaching ability may require addressing a variety of critical questions. Why do I want to teach? Why is teaching important today? Why do I believe in myself as a teacher? Why is teaching young people a valuable thing to do, especially when I see that it is such hard work? Once such fundamental questions have been answered and a commitment to the profession has been made, a teacher will be able to deal effectively with the periodic frustrations of classroom management.

## Beyond Classroom Management

Underlying all that we have said is our belief that becoming a teacher is a noble endeavor that takes time, energy, and professional commitment. One of the keys to becoming a teacher seems to be the degree to which the individual remains a life-long learner. Learning—about one's emotions, one's students, school environments, curricular developments—makes teaching a profession requiring continuous self-improvement and learning.

Teachers who are drained of energy and emotionally burned out often are those who have stopped learning, who have tried to remain the same year after year. They have discovered that teaching requires a lot of "giving," perhaps more than they are willing to give, and they try to give less instead of "getting" more —new materials, skills, activities, modes of presentation. Many years ago Kahlil Gibran wrote the following: "Whoever would be a teacher, let him begin by teaching himself before teaching others, and let him teach by example before teaching by word. For he who teaches himself and rectifies his own ways is more deserving of respect and reverence than he who would teach others and rectify their ways."[8] We who discuss "rectifying the

---

[8] Joseph Sheban, ed., *The Wisdom of Gibran* (New York: Bantam Books, 1973), p. 93.

ways" of students must complete our own studies first. Then we can look to the future, not with fear of ever-worsening classroom management problems, but with understanding based on knowledge, realistic expectations, sensitivity to students' needs and, hopefully, a touch of imagination.

# RESOURCE
# GUIDE

# Assertive Discipline

| | |
|---|---|
| *Key:* | Rules and consequences |
| *Slogan:* | Say what you mean and mean what you say |
| *Central Assumptions:* | Teacher attitudes govern teacher behavior |
| *Goal:* | Allow teacher to spend as much time teaching as possible |
| *Important Aspects:* | Student involvement in rule making |
| | Consequences for rule breaking are public |
| | Consequences range from a warning (name on board) to detention |
| | Teacher justifies disciplinary actions to students in terms of insistence on being able to teach |
| *Potential Problems:* | Little provision for out-of-class behavior problems |
| | Students depend on the teacher to resolve all problems |
| | Little opportunity for collaborative conflict resolution or exploration of origins of problems |

# Assertive Discipline

## For further information:

Canter and Associates, Inc.

P.O. Box 64517                    or                    1553 Euclid Street
Los Angeles, CA 90064                               Santa Monica, CA 90404
                                                            213-395-3221

## Selected References:

Canter, Lee (with Marlene Canter). *Assertive Discipline for Parents* (New York: Harper & Row, Publishers, 1983).

_____. *Assertive Discipline: A Take-Charge Approach for Today's Educator* (Los Angeles, Calif.: Canter and Associates, Inc., 1979).

Canter, Lee. "Taking Charge of Student Behavior." *National Elementary Principal*, Vol. 58, no. 4 (June 1979): 33–36, 41.

_____. "Competency-Based Approach to Discipline—It's Assertive." *Thrust for Educational Leadership*, Vol. 8, no. 3 (January 1979): 11–13.

# Behavior Modification

| | |
|---|---|
| *Key:* | Reinforcement |
| *Central Assumption:* | Students misbehave because the consequences of misbehavior are reinforcing |
| *Goals:* | Decrease negative behavior |
| | Increase positive behavior |
| *Important Aspects:* | Rewarding desirable behavior is more effective than punishing undesirable behavior |
| | Ignore attention-seeking misconduct |
| | Avoid expecting dramatic changes in behavior |
| *Potential Problems:* | Not all misbehavior may be attention seeking |
| | Behavior modification overlooks an understanding of the root causes of behavior problems |
| | Finding adequate reinforcers for older students may be difficult |

# Behavior Modification

## Selected References:

Clarizio, Harvey F. *Toward Positive Classroom Discipline*, 2nd ed. (New York: John Wiley & Sons, 1976).

Drabman, Ronald S., et al. "The Use and Misuse of Extinction in Classroom Behavioral Programs," *Psychology in the Schools*, Vol. 13, no. 4 (October 1976): 470–475.

Jenson, William R. "Behavior Modification in Secondary Schools: A Review," *Journal of Research and Development in Education*, Vol. 11, no. 5 (Summer 1978): 53–63.

Sloane, Howard N. *Classroom Management* (New York: John Wiley & Sons, 1976).

Thoresen, Carl, ed. *Behavior Modification in Education*. The Seventy-second Yearbook of the National Society for the Study of Education (Chicago: The University of Chicago Press, 1973).

Walker, Hill M., and Holland, Francine. "Issues, Strategies and Perspectives in the Management of Disruptive Child Behavior in the Classroom," *Journal of Education*, Vol. 161, no. 2 (Spring 1979): 25–50.

# Logical Consequences

| | |
|---|---|
| *Key:* | Student responsibility |
| *Goals:* | Replace punishments with consequences |
| | Encourage responsible behavior |
| *Central Assumptions:* | Student behavior is goal-directed |
| | Students learn best through concrete experiences |
| *Important Aspects:* | For individual problems, confront students with diagnosis (attention, power, revenge, display of weakness) |
| | For classroom and school problems, involve students in rule making |
| | Establish logical consequences for rule breaking |
| | In resolving conflicts, teachers should not fight or give in |
| *Potential Problems:* | Possibility that teacher will misdiagnose an individual problem |
| | Interventions are clinical in nature and require time |
| | Logical consequences are difficult to develop and sometimes impossible to impose |

# Logical Consequences

## For further information:

North American Society of
Adlerian Psychology
159 North Deerborn
Chicago, Illinois 60601
312-346-3458

Dr. John Platt
Elk Grove Unified School District
8820 Elk Grove Boulevard
Elk Grove, California 95624
916-685-9269

## Selected References:

Dreikurs, Rudolf. *Psychology in the Classroom: A Manual for Teachers* (New York: Harper & Row, 1957).

Dreikurs, Rudolf, and Cassel, Pearl. *Discipline Without Tears*, 2nd ed. (New York: Hawthorn Books, 1972).

Dreikurs, Rudolf, and Grey, Loren. *A New Approach to Discipline: Logical Consequences* (New York: Hawthorn Books, 1968).

Dreikurs, Rudolf, Grunwald, Bernice, and Pepper, Floy C. *Maintaining Sanity in the Classroom: Classroom Management Techniques* (New York: Harper & Row, 1982).

## Positive Peer Culture

| | |
|---|---|
| *Key:* | Peer support |
| *Central Assumptions:* | Problems are normal |
| | Troubled students can help themselves by first helping others |
| *Goal:* | Provide opportunities for students to help each other |
| *Important Aspects:* | Single-sex groups of nine troubled students and one adult leader |
| | New members spend first meetings working on others' problems |
| | Each meeting focuses on one student's concerns |
| *Potential Problems:* | The process is time-consuming |
| | It is unsuited to on-the-spot intervention |
| | Group leaders must make a long-term commitment |

# Positive Peer Culture

## For further information:

Harry Vorrath, President
Center for Group Studies
Route 1, Box 136
Shenandoah, Virginia 22849
703-652-6053

## Selected References:

James, Howard. *Children in Trouble: A National Scandal* (New York: Pocket Books, 1971). Reprint from the *Christian Science Monitor*.

Vorrath, Harry H., and Brendtro, Larry K. *Positive Peer Culture* (Hawthorne, N.Y.: Aldine, 1979).

# Reality Therapy

| | |
|---|---|
| *Key:* | Self-awareness |
| *Central Assumption:* | Student behavior problems often derive from low self-esteem |
| *Goal:* | Increase opportunities for students to feel good about themselves |
| *Important Aspects:* | Create groups in which students can discuss concerns and develop communication and awareness skills |
| | Eliminate activities that ensure some students will "fail" |
| | See that students make a formal commitment to overcome problems |
| *Potential Problems:* | Students may need to learn to deal with failure in a positive way for later life |
| | Reality Therapy can be time-consuming |
| | Teachers must be careful not to manipulate group meetings or make them "unsafe" |

# Reality Therapy

## For further information:

Educator Training Center
100 East Ocean Boulevard, Suite 906
Long Beach, California 90802
213-435-7951

## Selected References:

Bassin, Alexander. "Reality Therapy in the Classroom," *Journal for Specialists in Group Work*, Vol. 3, no. 2 (Summer 1978): 63–77.

Bourgeois, Don. "Positive Discipline: A Practical Approach to Disruptive Behavior," *NASSP Bulletin*, Vol. 63, no. 428 (September 1979): 68–71.

Glasser, William. *Schools Without Failure* (New York: Harper & Row, 1969).

_____. *Reality Therapy* (New York: Harper & Row, 1975).

_____. "Ten Steps to Good Discipline," *Today's Education*, Vol. 66, no. 4 (November–December 1977): 61–63.

Lipman, Victor. "Mr. Glasser's Gentle Rod," *American Education*, Vol. 14, no. 7 (August–September 1978): 28–31.

National Education Association. "Reality Therapy. Description of Teacher Inservice Education Materials" (Washington, D.C.: National Education Association, 1977).

Rich, John Martin. "Glasser and Kohl: How Effective Are Their Strategies to Discipline?" *NASSP Bulletin*, Vol. 63, no. 428 (September 1979): 19–26.

# Social Literacy Training

| | |
|---|---|
| *Key:* | Open communications |
| *Slogan:* | "Speak true words about central conflicts" |
| *Central Assumptions:* | Classrooms provide few opportunities for open honest communications |
| *Goal:* | "No-lose" conflict resolution |
| *Important Aspects:* | Consciousness-raising activities designed to reveal student and teacher concerns |
| | Teachers share responsibility for resolving conflicts with students |
| *Potential Problems:* | Problem resolution can be time-consuming |
| | The process is unsuited to on-the-spot intervention |
| | Some students may not take conflict-resolution "games" seriously |

# Social Literacy Training

## For further information:

Dr. Alfred S. Alschuler
456 Hills South
University of Massachusetts at Amherst
Amherst, Massachusetts 01003
413-545-2047

## Selected References:

Alschuler, Alfred S. *School Discipline: A Socially Literate Solution* (New York: McGraw-Hill, 1980).

Alschuler, Alfred, et al. "Social Literacy: A Discipline Game Without Losers," *Phi Delta Kappan*, Vol. 58, no. 8 (April 1977): 606–609.

*Also Available:*

"Resolving Classroom Conflict Through Social Literacy," Eight Audio-Tape Workshops. Order from National Education Association Publishing, Room 609, 1201 16th St., N.W., Washington, D.C. 20036 (202-833-4233).

# Systematic Management Plan for School Discipline

| | |
|---|---|
| *Key:* | Organizational change |
| *Central Assumptions:* | Problems are endemic to schools |
| | Organizational factors determine behavior |
| | Comprehensive — not piecemeal — change |
| *Goals:* | Address student behavior on a schoolwide basis |
| | Establish organizational mechanisms for reducing problems |
| *Important Aspects:* | Understanding the school as a rule-governed organization |
| | Data collection |
| | Conflict resolution |
| | Team troubleshooting |
| | Parental involvement |
| | Reinforcing environments for learning |
| | Professional development |
| *Potential Problems:* | Requires careful coordination |
| | SMPSD can be time-consuming |
| | Commitment of resources may be necessary |

# Systematic Management Plan
## for School Discipline

## For further information:

Daniel Duke, Director
Education Administration Program
Lewis and Clark College
Portland, Oregon 97219

Adrienne Meckel
c/o School of Education
Stanford University
Stanford, Calif. 94305

## Selected References:

Duke, Daniel L. "A Systematic Management Plan for School Discipline,"
*NAASP Bulletin*, Vol. 61, no. 405 (January 1977): 1–10.
———, ed. *Classroom Management*, The Seventy-eighth Yearbook of the
National Society for the Study of Education, Part 11 (Chicago: University of Chicago Press, 1979).
Duke, Daniel L., and Meckel, Adrienne M. *Managing Student Behavior
Problems* (New York: Teachers College Press, 1980).

# Teacher Effectiveness Training

| | |
|---|---|
| *Key:* | Teacher communications |
| *Central Assumptions:* | No one can be *forced* to do anything |
| | Problems cannot be totally eliminated |
| *Goals:* | "No-lose" conflict resolution |
| | Less provocative teacher talk |
| *Important Aspects:* | "I" messages |
| | "Owning" the problem |
| | Six-step problem-resolution process |
| | Active listening |
| *Potential Problems:* | Problem resolution can be time-consuming |
| | Teachers may have to change their values on occasion |
| | Students may "test" the negotiations process |

# Teacher Effectiveness Training

*For further information:*

Teacher Effectiveness Information
Effectiveness Training Incorporated
531 Stevens Avenue
Solano Beach, Calif. 92075
714-481-8121

## Selected References:

Gordon, Thomas. *T.E.T.: Teacher Effectiveness Training* (New York: Peter H. Wyden, 1974).
Ligon, Jerry. "How to Run a Needs Meeting," *Clearing House*, Vol. 52, no. 7 (March 1979): 336–339.

# Transactional Analysis

| | |
|---|---|
| *Key:* | Interpersonal communications |
| *Central Assumptions:* | People have three ego states: child, parent, and adult |
| | Problems arise when people interact on basis of different ego states |
| *Goal:* | Understand the gamelike nature of communications |
| *Important Aspects:* | Clinical contacts between teacher and student |
| | Active listening |
| | Awareness of origins of behavior |
| *Potential Problems:* | The process can be time-consuming |
| | Teachers may feel discomfort in a "clinical" role |
| | Potential harm if follow-up is not provided |

# Transactional Analysis

## For further information:

Information Services Department
International Transactional Analysts Association
1772 Vallejo Street
San Francisco, Calif. 94123
415-885-5992

## Selected References:

Berne, Eric. *Games People Play* (New York: Grove Press, 1964.).

Bourgeois, Don. "Positive Discipline: A Practical Approach to Disruptive Behavior," *NASSP Bulletin*, Vol. 63, no. 428 (September 1979): 68–71.

Ernst, Ken. *Games Students Play* (Millbrae, Calif.: Celestial Arts, 1975).

James, Muriel, and Jongeward, Muriel. *The People Book* (Menlo Park, Calif.: Addison-Wesley, 1975).

Kravas, Konstantinos J., and Kravas, Constance H. "Transactional Analysis for Classroom Management," *Phi Delta Kappan*, Vol. 56, no. 3 (November 1974): 194–197.

Woollams, Stan, and Brown, Michael. *TA, the Total Handbook of Transactional Analysis* (Englewood Cliffs, N. J.: Prentice-Hall, 1979).

## General References

American School Board Association. "Are Our Schools Creating Drug Abusers?" *American School Board Journal*, Vol. 161, no. 1 (January 1974): 12–13.

Blum, Richard H. *Drug Education: Results and Recommendations* (Lexington, Mass.: D. C. Heath & Company, 1976).

Coates, Thomas J., and Thoresen, Carl E. "Teacher Anxiety: A Review with Recommendations," *Review of Educational Research*, Vol. 45, no. 3 (Spring 1976): 159–184.

Doyle, Walter. "Classroom Management and Teacher Decision Making." Paper presented at the American Educational Research Association meeting, San Francisco, April 1979.

Duke, Daniel L. "Adults Can Be Discipline Problems Too!" *Psychology in the Schools*, Vol. 15, no. 4 (October 1978): 522–528.

_____. "How Administrators View the Crisis in School Discipline," *Phi Delta Kappan*, Vol. 59, no. 5 (January 1978): 325–330.

_____, ed. *Classroom Management* (Chicago: University of Chicago Press, 1979).

Duke, Daniel L. and Meckel, Adrienne M. "The Slow Death of a Public High School," *Phi Delta Kappan*, Vol. 61, no. 10 (June 1980): 674–677.

_____. "Student Attendance Problems and School Organization: A Case Study," *Urban Education*, Vol. 15, no. 3 (October 1980): 325–357.

Educational Research, Inc. "Drug Education: Goals, Approaches, Evaluation" (Arlington, Va.: Educational Research Service, Inc., 1975).

Engs, Ruth C. *Responsible Drug and Alcohol Use* (New York: Macmillan Publishing Company, 1979).

James, Howard. *Children in Trouble: A National Scandal* (New York: Pocket Books, 1971).

Lortie, Dan C. *Schoolteacher* (Chicago: The University of Chicago Press, 1975).

Moos, Rudolf H., ed. *Human Adaptation: Coping with Life Crises* (Lexington, Mass.: D. C. Heath & Co., 1976).

National Institute of Education. *Violent Schools — Safe Schools*, The Safe School Study Report to the Congress, Vol. I (Washington, D.C.: National Institute of Education, 1978).

National Institute on Drug Abuse. *National Institute on Drug Abuse Report* (Washington, D.C.: Department of Health, Education and Welfare, 1980).

Reutter, Edmund. *The Courts and Student Conduct* (Topeka, Kan.: The National Organization on Legal Problems of Education, 1975).

Sheban, Joseph, ed. *The Wisdom of Gibran* (New York: Bantam Books, 1973).

Yankelovich, Daniel. "How Students Control Their Drug Crisis," *Psychology Today*, October 1975, pp. 39–42.

# I · N · D · E · X

## About the Authors

DANIEL L. DUKE is professor of educational administration and director of the Educational Administration Program at Lewis and Clark College in Portland, Oregon. His professional experiences encompass high school teaching and administration, organization of an alternative school, and design of the Stanford University Instructional Leadership Program. Recent research and writing have focused on classroom management and school discipline, school effectiveness, and the role of the principal as instructional leader. Among his books are *Managing Student Behavior Problems* (with Adrienne Meckel), *Classroom Management* (the Seventy-ninth Yearbook of the National Society for the Study of Education), and *Helping Teachers Manage Classrooms*. Soon to be published is a book on the future of teaching entitled *Teaching — The Imperiled Profession*. Professor Duke lives with his wife Cheryl and children Devan, Jay, Joshua, and Krista in Tigard, Oregon.

ADRIENNE MARAVICH MECKEL is an evaluation consultant for the Stanford Teacher Education Program, Stanford University. A graduate of the University of Southern California, she has earned Masters degrees from Chapman College, the Monterey Institute, and Stanford University and a Ph.D in curriculum development and teacher education from Stanford University. She has taught at the junior high, high school, and college levels and was program administrator of the Stanford Teacher Education Program in 1980–1981. Previous publications with Dr. Duke include *Managing Student Behavior Problems* and "The Slow Death of a Public High School." She lives in Carmel Valley, California, with her husband and daughter.